TEAMS THAT SWEAR

ADRIAN BAILLARGEON

Editing and proofreading by Cavalletti Communications, www.cavacom.biz

Cover design, illustrations and typesetting by Self-publishing Lab, www.selfpublishinglab.com

Cover concept by Lucy Coggan
Author photograph by Rebecca Taylor, rebeccataylor.com.au

ISBN:

Hardcover 978-0-6488754-8-2
Paperback 978-0-6488754-2-0
E-book 978-0-6488754-5-1

Foreword

Being able to connect and work together as humans is incredibly important. It can be difficult at times and it can be easy at times – but it's never the same. A new team member equals a new team and therefore finding ways to connect and work together is a fundamental skill. This is a challenge that Adrian Baillargeon knows well.

I first met Adrian whilst I was working with Cricket Australia, leading the high performance program from our base at the National Cricket Centre in Brisbane. Adrian was working with Bupa, who became our naming rights partner; it didn't take me long to realise Adrian had some great insights and a clear passion for creating effective teams. This was the start of a journey that continues today as we stay connected and share challenges, podcasts and readings with the goal of improving leadership and team performance.

What has been my experience working with others to achieve a common goal? Taking a step right back in time, I recently stumbled across my kindergarten report card written by Mrs Rogers, my first teacher at Werris Creek Primary School; she wrote: "Belinda enjoys school. She is a loving thoughtful little girl, sensitive to others and happy to be able to help everyone. Belinda responds well to responsibility and enjoys leadership." Sure my father was the Principal at the time, but let's ignore any bias! And then at age 12, from my sixth class report: "Belinda is a hardworking, reliable pupil.

Leadership qualities have been most apparent throughout the year." This time from Hamilton South Public School in Newcastle, where Dad wasn't the Principal (phew).

I had a lucky start with a strong family unit and great teachers who provided me opportunities to play with the abstract concepts of leadership and teamwork, but cricket was the vehicle for me to really learn about them.

Thrust into the role of Captain of the Australian Team at age 23, I started on a journey and fascination that continues today. High-level sport simplifies the concept of teamwork beautifully: The goal is clear, roles are defined, contribution is expected, feedback is demanded, and everyone benefits if you succeed – the desire to be better is high. BUT ... you must get the relationships humming if your team is to succeed, and this is the challenging part.

In my experience, when teams are comfortable challenging each other for the betterment of the team's performance something special happens, like when my team won World Cups in 1997 and 2005. Likewise, when the relationships are not quite right, where self-interest starts to raise its head, when things are left unsaid – then you are on a slippery slope, which is also something I experienced under my leadership. It was in fact under these circumstance that I learnt the most. The ability to reflect, learn and try again are as important as having a go in the first place.

Transferring what I learnt on the sporting field into a professional environment was a real test for me and something I still enjoy the challenge of today. The mission is not always as clear, the ambiguity is higher, and onboarding hearts and minds into the mission from a diverse range of people and perspectives can be much more challenging than on the sporting field. Building a team is something you need to work at daily.

This book, *Teams That Swear*, provides a great summary of the research into building—as Adrian says—teams that shine. It also provides wonderful examples, drawn from Adrian's long experience, that bring the key elements of great teams to life. The simplicity of Adrian's Higher Performing Teams Model provides a strong framework. However, it is the simple, practical activities that will help leaders and teams from all works of life play with what is one of life's great joys – being in a team that swears by each other.

Belinda Clark AO
Former Captain of *Australia's Women's World Cup Champion Cricket Teams and Sports Executive*
August 2020

TEAMS THAT SWEAR

ADRIAN BAILLARGEON

Contents

How this book can help leaders and their teams

NASA lost their Mars Climate Orbiter, costing the program millions of dollars. A state police department in Australia faked over 250,000 alcohol breath tests. A one-time Atlanta Falcons coach rode with his captain in a Bentley instead of the team bus to a bowling game. And employees from one of Australia's biggest banks fraudulently used kids' bank accounts to hit targets.

Not exactly great examples of teams doing 'together' better. However, other teams have. One team embraced the neurodiversity of its team members to increase the group's effectiveness. One of the greatest bands on earth embraced feedback that then propelled them to global icon status. And a sporting team that had not won a championship in 108 years finally broke its curse; it took red wine, cowboy hats and an old man wearing thick glasses to bring the team together.

All these examples demonstrate what is possible when teams do together well or when they don't do it so well. When together is done well, meaningful progress can be made. When together is not done well, it can cost billions of dollars and no small amount of mental pain.

Working in teams is like listening to music. When you're working in a bad team, it's like listening to a song that drives you bonkers. Can you think of one right now? Got it? I have mine. It's annoying.

I want nothing to do with it. I want to turn it off and switch to a different one. It's the same when you work in a bad team. You switch off. You can't stand it. And you want to leave.

Now, think of your favourite song. How does it make you feel? Energetic? Happy? Does it make you do things you may not normally do, like sing out at the top of your lungs? This is what it's like when you are part of a great team. Exciting. Engaging. You walk with a little extra hop in your step. And you may even feel more comfortable doing things you are not used to.

For me, that song is Toto's 'Africa'. I love it. And who doesn't want to work in a team they love? Unfortunately, there's not a lot of 'Africa' or other great songs playing in the background in many workplaces. The 2017 Gallup 'State of the Global Workplace' report showed that only 31% of North Americans, 24% of Australians and just 10% of Western Europeans are engaged at work.[1] That's a good chunk of the global workforce that's disengaged. CPP Global estimated in 2008 that US$359 billion of lost productivity per year was due to unresolved workplace conflict in America.[2] In Australia in 2010, the Productivity Commission estimated that the cost of workplace bullying alone was $36 billion annually.[3] These are staggering numbers.

Our health is also impacted by the way we work together. In the period between 2012 and 2017, each year on average 7,140 Australians were compensated for work-related mental health conditions.[4] Of the serious mental health claims where workers missed over a week of work, most of them (92%) were associated with work-related mental stress[5] and over half (58%) of those claims were categorised as harassment, bullying or work pressure.[6] The cost to businesses—and their customers—in mental health compensation claims is approximately $543 million per year.[7]

Why is doing together better so hard today?

Customer expectations are higher than ever. Customers are like kids waiting to open their presents from Santa – they can't wait. They want things now and in a way that's convenient for them. They no longer just purchase on price or product – it's also about the customer experience and what the company stands for. This means organisations must work harder than ever to keep customers happy. Working harder can increase stress levels, leading to unpleasant and quite simply, unacceptable behaviours.

From a people perspective, we now work with a much broader range of cultures, generations and working arrangements. Working from home, part-time hours, flexible hours, compressed workweeks, job-sharing and other new ways of working are emerging and evolving. We work globally. We are working later in our lives. All of which can add to communication challenges in the workplace.

Technology advancements have created a double-edged sword. I can see and talk to my buddy Al in Saskatoon while I am eating breakfast across from the Sydney Opera House, and at the same time receive eight emails – including three from my boss sent the night before. This is good – and bad.

It's obvious organisations are challenged every day to keep up, break down silos and bring people together to deliver in a productive manner. We work with more uncertainty, stress and quite frankly unhappy people than ever before. In a world where technology connects us more than ever, the human connection at work seems to be drifting away.

The possibilities for teams are endless

The good news is that there has never been a better time for leaders to rise to the top and lead their teams. Apple, Airbnb, Uber, Tesla and Netflix are just a few examples that demonstrate what's possible when teams perform well, and their successes have inspired many people and organisations around the world. These companies are often held as the gold standard for collaboration, disruption and new ways of working. On the flip side, I hear that some of their leaders are not always the gold standard for working well with others. If this is true, I can't help but wonder if some of their leadership skills were stronger—particularly empathy, humility and emotional intelligence—how much more of an impact these leaders and their teams could have.

When it comes to working together as teams, Reid Hoffman, co-founder of LinkedIn sums it up best: "No matter how brilliant your mind or strategy, if you're playing a solo game, you'll always lose out to a team."

And that is why I have written this book. To help brilliant minds and strategies come together through the power of human interaction and teamwork. I want to help people do *together* better.

Teams That Swear was written with:

1. The knowledge of what it's really like to work in a fast-paced, complicated work environment. I've worked in organisations with as few as 12 employees all the way up to 24,000, led teams of 1 and teams of 47. The experiences I share in this book are all presented through the lens of what really works in the workplace.

2. The belief that by working together, putting your team's agenda ahead of your own and contributing to a greater good, is the way to make meaningful progress.
3. The assumption that people can change, and through the power of dialogue and action, organisations can change.
4. The belief it can all start with one person believing in something simple yet powerful. And that belief is that we can do together better.

So why can't that person be me? Or you? Or better yet – why can't it be 'we'?

Leading teams, leading change and getting people aligned can be hard work. It can keep you awake at night. At times—sometimes many times—you will ask yourself, why do I do this? The answer is because you can. And we need you to. Because we need great leaders. Great leaders have the ability to inspire, make wonderful things happen, and have an impact that lasts a lifetime. For some, it may come naturally. For others—like me—you have to work at it, stumble and pick yourself up again. The best leaders I've worked with, seen in action and interviewed all said they struggled, screwed up and found it hard. But they persevered and were able to succeed by working at doing together better. They took *deliberate* steps to make themselves, their people and their teams better.

According to Dr Seuss, "The more that you read, the more things you will know, the more that you learn, the more places you'll go."

That's what I want this book to be about. I hope you'll go to more places by putting some of what I share into action.

When I set out to write this book, I wanted readers to benefit in at least three ways:

1. To help people *reflect* on their approaches and actions and identify what they might do differently as a result of what is shared in this book.
2. To help people *take deliberate steps* to realise more of the potential of working together.
3. To *inspire* new ways of doing together better. These new ways may come directly from this book, or a new idea may spark from something you've read here.

Who will benefit from this book

The earliest human fossils found to date are over 200,000 years old.* That's a long time to be figuring out how to work together. As a human society we've done alright to survive. We've probably got quite a bit worked out about how to work together. However, sometimes we forget and have a brain fart. Or a situation causes us to act differently than what's ideal.

So how the heck is this book going to help?

For experienced leaders, it could serve as a refresher. After attending one of my talks to nearly 600 of his employees, the hosting GM said to me, "You have certainly sparked a few things for me, emphasised things I already know ... Unfortunately, I let work get in the way of the things I already know." I've got a sneaking

---

* Assuming you are reading this book in the 21st century.

suspicion we all let work get in the way of doing things better. So one way to use this book is as a spark. A reminder. To not let work get in the way, and to refocus on what you already know.

For new leaders – please feel free to use as many of the ideas, stories, questions and activities in this book as you please. I've shared them for exactly this reason. Steal with pride my friends!

For aspiring leaders – avoid waiting for the 'leader' title to use what you learn. You may be leading a project, you may be leading a component of a project, or you might 'simply' be a team member. It doesn't matter. Everything shared in the book is just as applicable to you as it is for nominated leaders.

How to use this book

Teams That Swear is divided into four main sections. The first section identifies what's been proven to work in high performing teams. Throughout this section, I'll share what I've learned from years of research, insights I've garnered from leaders around the world and learnings from my own experiences.

The second section provides you with the opportunity to diagnose where your team is at. You'll learn about the characteristics of high performing teams (teams that are shining) and less-than-ideal performing teams.

In the third and fourth sections you will find ideas and tips to help get or keep your team shining. To help your team swear *by* each other rather than *about* each other.

How to get the best out of your reading

When reading this book, be involved. Remember that famous saying by Benjamin Franklin, "Tell me and I'll forget, teach me and I may remember, involve me and I'll learn." When reading *Teams That Swear*, have a pen or pencil with you, or use the highlighting or annotation function on your device. If something resonates with you, highlight it. If you want to come back to something, circle it. If you love something – take a photo of it and share it on social media. If you disagree with something – take a photo and post it on social media. If you think someone in your team will like it, take a photo and flick it to them. As much as I hope this book entertains, provokes and motivates, I want it to inspire action over time. I'll share stories you may want to incorporate into your storytelling; I'll share statistics and case studies you may want to use when creating your case for change; and I'll share some exercises you may want to try with your teams.

English Philosopher Francis Bacon once said, "A prudent question is one-half of wisdom." At the end of each chapter, I will ask you some questions. I encourage you to take the time to answer them – in your head or in this book. This way we are working together to come up with the wisdom. The questions have been designed to help you reflect on your past experiences, incorporate new learnings and come up with an action plan to do together better.

If the first half of wisdom, according to Bacon, is asking prudent questions, I think the second half is having an idea about what the answer to those prudent questions might be. A great mentor of mine, Miles Callaghan, who has held various senior leadership positions across the pharmaceutical, insurance and aged care industries, once suggested I was missing opportunities to make a difference. He wanted me to share my thoughts more often. He said to me, "If you don't speak up and share your opinion, you aren't adding value to the meeting." It's not just Miles who thinks this. Research backs this up too, which I'll share with you later.

This is where you come in. Just as Miles suggested to me, I encourage you to share your opinion. Then take your learning one step further. Put that opinion into practice within a week to make your team better. Take one deliberate step to be better, to be different and to move forward. Ralph Waldo Emerson said, "Don't be too timid and squeamish about your action. All life is an experiment." Experiment, experiment, experiment.

That's enough talk – let's get into the action. Good luck!

Acknowledgements

Everything that you'll read in this book is the result of many people who have influenced me in innumerable ways. They have been generous with their time and insights, and I am lucky to have had them as part of my teams over the years.

My Shining Team
My wife Noodle, and our children Jack, Oli and Ryan
Mom, Dad, Shane and Steven

My Coaches
Coach Hanson, Arty, Bronsy, Worl, DJ and Coach C (there were many more so I apologise in advance to all my coaches not mentioned here who have helped me along the way).

My Leaders
Les, Liz, Jim, Shane, Alison, Arthur, John, Smithy, Miles, Eric, Cassius, Jane and John.

My Teams
Too many to list, but you all know who you are and I thank you all for the ups, downs and in-betweens. I am thankful for the great times we had and the fantastic things we made happen.

Story Contributors

Many people have contributed their experiences and insights, for this book and over the years, for which I am grateful.

Miles Callaghan
Mr Cam Carter
Heidi Clarris
Lucy Coggan
Ben Darwin
Scott Dinsdale
Colin D Ellis
Simon Gaymer
Douglas Isles
Carly Loder
Glenn Stewart
Simon Strachan
Tim Williams

About me

I have been called many things. Some I like, others I am not too sure about. At times I have been referred to as a behavioural consultant, a team leadership coach and my colleagues' biggest supporter. Whatever you want to call me, one thing is for certain. I am passionate about helping leaders make meaningful progress through the power of their people.

My career (and life) started in Saskatoon, Saskatchewan,* Canada. Saskatchewan lays claim to cold winters, 100,000 lakes, the Saskatchewan Roughriders and Joni Mitchell. After completing a degree in Marketing and Finance at the University of Saskatchewan, I spent the first 19 years of my career in the corporate, community and sport environments across Canada and Australia, as well as some coaching in Cameroon and Tunisia. I've worked in health and care, financial services, insurance, pharmaceuticals, oil and gas, and the beverage industry. I've been part of teams in marketing, sales, HR, risk and joint venture management.

Sport, music and movies have always been big parts of my life, and you'll find examples from all of these areas woven throughout the book. These three components of my life have inspired me, challenged me, and made me think about what kind of person and leader I want to be. From coaching the under-14 Bantam B

---

* Despite popular belief, the Sasquatch did not originate in Saskatchewan.

Blue Jays team to starting a Tball Smash program for our local community, I've been drawn to making a positive impact through kids and sport. As a coach in Douala and Yaoundé in Cameroon and Tunis in Tunisia on behalf of Major League Baseball, I had the opportunity to work with teams across different language and cultural environments. Baseball is funny – it's a game where if you fail 7 out of 10 times over your career when hitting, you are considered one of the best ever to play. The game has taught me a lot about teamwork, self-belief and resilience, and how to manage a broad set of personalities.

Music and movies also resonate with me strongly. I have turned to them in good times and bad, and they have provided inspiration and created bonds between me and my children. Song lyrics can be a source of truth, guidance and confirmation when we need them most. One of the most powerful exercises I've used when working with teams is to ask team members to find a lyric that resonates with them that they can draw upon during challenging times. It's another way music has given me a little glimpse into the human psyche.

Just like music, movies can make a positive impact on our lives. Whether it's the storyline, a character, a certain scene or just one line, movies can remind us about "all that once was good and could be again", as James Earl Jones's character Terrence Mann says in my favourite movie, *Field of Dreams*. Burt Lancaster's character 'Moonlight' Doc Graham from the same movie is one for the ages. As he tells Kevin Costner's character, "Sometimes we just don't recognise life's most significant moments while they're happening. Back then I thought, 'Well, there'll be other days'. I didn't realise that that was the only day." I often think about this line when the two voices in my head are debating whether or not to take on an opportunity. As we progress through this book, I refer to various movie scenes and characters to help bring a point alive. I hope you enjoy them.

There have been two common threads throughout my professional career. The first is leading teams of all shapes and sizes; I've seen what works and what doesn't. The second is working closely with external departments and external teams. From managing a joint venture, leading multimillion-dollar sponsorship relationships and working with sales, marketing, finance, HR, legal, IT and risk teams, I've been fortunate to work with many people 'outside' my team to achieve a common goal.

I am now an author, keynote speaker, facilitator and coach. I am a true believer in the power of teams. I believe when you get a group of people working well together, meaningful progress can be made to make our world a better place.

The power of a swear word

Saskatoon is a relatively small, yet very proud, city. With a population of over 270,000, it's a place where you can get anywhere in 15 minutes. We endure (and survive) long cold winters where the temperatures can dip into the –40s (yes that's Celsius).

Growing up, I had two brothers, a mum and a dad. Eventually we convinced our parents we needed to get a dog named Gypsy.

Mom* and Dad quickly helped us learn what it was like to work in a team. We all played team sports. We also learned early on how to share the work around the house. I vividly remember picking weeds in the back alley of our house on Cascade Street. This job seemed to come up more often when we were older and had been out late the night before. First thing Saturday morning, Mom and Dad would have us out in the alley with a table knife each, picking weeds and making our section of the back alley look good. Pitching in, taking pride in our surroundings and learning by doing were important to my parents.

Throughout my childhood I rarely heard my parents swear in front of us. Which is quite impressive when you think about all the chaos three young boys would have caused. My poor mum had to put up with us bickering over important issues such as who would play Ice Hockey on the Nintendo next. Yet I can't recall her using any well-deserved expletives. She later shared with me that she

---

* In Canada we say 'mom' and in Australia we say 'mum', so in this book my (Canadian) mum is 'Mom' to me!

associated swearing with anger and didn't feel it was right to swear in front of us, no matter how much frustration we may have caused.

During my summers while I was at university, Dad got me a job working at the same industrial plumbing and heating company where he worked. During those summers on the job site, swearing was the norm. For Dad to be in that environment every day and not bring it home was impressive.

However, I have learned that when it comes to working with people (using tools or not), swearing seems to have some sort of profound effect. I have often heard people say, 'I swear by this approach' or 'I swear that's what I heard', and of course the old classic, 'I swear on my mother's grave'.

When I moved to Australia in 2005, I noticed swearing was much more part of the regular conversation. I would crown the term 'bloody' as the great Aussie adjective. Encouraging drivers not to drink and drive, TAC, a state-based government agency whose responsibilities include promoting road safety, used the tagline, 'If you drink, then drive, you're a bloody idiot' in a wide-reaching campaign to reduce drinking and driving. Tourism Australia also jumped into the swearing game with the now-infamous 2006 'So Where The Bloody Hell Are You?' campaign.

It's not just the 'softer' swear words Aussies are comfortable with. Arguably the harshest word (it's a four-letter word, starts with the letter C and rhymes with 'runt') seems to be used as a term of endearment. When playing indoor cricket, I'd often hear 'Good on ya, c _ _ _'. Or in a tongue in cheek manner, 'Ah, shut up c _ _ _'. Full on, isn't it?

At work—in the corporate space—I experienced a similar use of profanities. Not as many C bombs, probably more F bombs. Some people were happy to drop an F bomb here and there. F that person, F the business, F the project, F the budget, F me! I worked with a great colleague who was very comfortable using this type of language. I playfully flagged my observations to her one day and so the debate began about whether swearing was good or bad.

Being somewhat competitive, I felt research would support my argument that swearing isn't good. Much to my bloody disgust, I was proven wrong. Cognitive psychologist Kristin Janschewitz, Associate Professor at Marist College in New York, has found evidence that suggests there is no proven harm in the impacts of swearing. Having observed over 10,000 episodes of swearing in public—with adults and kiddos—her work suggests that most uses of swear words are not problematic. Swearing doesn't lead to acts of violence, and for most people swearing leads to positive outcomes. Swearing to make people laugh for example, is quite common.

Janschewitz also noted that swearing can help achieve a number of positive outcomes "when used positively for joking or storytelling, stress management, fitting in with the crowd, or as a substitute for physical aggression".[8]

Ok, so swearing doesn't cause any harm if used the right way. But it actually helps and is good for me? There was still a part of me that didn't quite feel right about what I had discovered so I dug a little deeper. And to my colleague's delight, the case got stronger for her. Here's what I discovered:

- Swearing can increase an individual's pain threshold. Psychologist Richard Stephens at Keele University in Staffordshire in England discovered people could keep their hands submerged in ice water about 50% longer when they swore compared to when they used a neutral word.[9]

- Move over steroids, swearing can make you stronger. Stephens performed two experiments that led him to this conclusion. The first involved a group jumping onto exercise bikes and riding for 30 seconds against a fair amount of resistance. The second involved participants challenged with a hand dynamometer (a squeezy type of thing) which measures grip strength. Surprise, surprise – both groups performed better when repeating swear words during the activity compared to repeating neutral words. F me! For the squeezers, the results were 8% better, while the cyclists' results were between 2% and 4% better.[10] Remember, all those one-percenters can make a difference.

- Swearing can relieve feelings of rejection or exclusion. In 2012 researchers at the University of Queensland asked 70 volunteers "to remember an experience of being excluded from a group or included in a group". Researchers asked one group to swear while retelling their stories, and another group to recount theirs without swearing. The group that included profanities in their stories reported lower feelings of social pain.[11]

- And finally, and more closely aligned to the arena of high performing teams, research from Australia and New Zealand has shown that "risking a swear word of frustration, amusement or sympathy among members of a new social group is an important barometer of how much we believe that our good intentions are accepted".[12] The researchers concluded that, "We tend to swear among those we trust, and swearing can help to create trust."[13] In an interview with *National Geographic*, Emma Byrne, author of *Swearing is Good for You*, summed up the research best when she said, "jocular abuse, particularly swearing among friends, is a strong signal of the degree of trust that those friends share. When you look at the transcripts of these case studies of effective teams in sectors like manufacturing and IT, those that can joke with each other in ways that transgress polite speech, which includes a lot of swearing, tend to report that they trust each other more."[14]

So does this mean that to create higher performing teams, rolling out a tirade of expletives is the way to go? Remember, words have an impact. Big impact. Look at this list of words and think about the impact they have had on our world:

'I have a dream'
'I love you'
'I h@te you' (the H word is deemed a swear word in our house)
'No'
#metoo
'Make love, not war'
'Please'
'Thank you'
'If you build it, he will come'

When it comes to swearing in teams, it's not necessarily what you say, it's how you say it. And when, and to whom, and where. Hence the name of this book: we're aiming to create teams that might swear *at* each other, but it's because they swear *by* each other. These are high performing teams.

SECTION 1

Different Perspectives of
Team Development

CHAPTER 1

History of team development

The year 1965 was an influential one for mankind. Civil rights activist Malcolm X was shot dead in New York City. Gen Xers were first born, including JK Rowling, who would go on to become one of the most popular writers of our time. McDonald's shares were listed publicly for the first time. The famous scene of Muhammad Ali towering over Sonny Liston was etched into history when Ali knocked out Liston in the first round with what is still known as the 'phantom punch'.[15] Earlier in the year, one of the most popular musical films of all time, The Sound of Music, starring Julie Andrews and Christopher Plummer, was released. In the music world, The Righteous Brothers' 'You've Lost That Lovin' Feeling' reached #1 on the charts. And perhaps not for the first time, the Rolling Stones were fined £5 each for public urination.[16]

When it comes to team dynamics, 1965 was also a big year. It marked the publication of Bruce Tuckman's popular theory of group dynamics. A PhD graduate of Princeton University, Tuckman's 'Developmental Sequence in Small Group' was published in the *Psychological Bulletin*. You may not recognise the name, but I suspect you will have heard of his stages of team development: Forming, Storming, Norming, Performing. And then in 1977 (a great year in the Baillargeon household, I might add), Adjourning was added as the fifth stage.

Tuckman characterised these five stages in the following way:

Forming:

- When teams first come together, they are typically in the Forming stage.
- Some team members are excited to start something new, others may be anxious as they might not be 100% clear on what the team will do.
- Most members are positive and polite. Politeness may be superficial as team members get a feel for each other.
- Time is spent getting to know each other but with limited personal disclosure. There is a feeling of 'Will I be accepted?' and 'Can I trust them?'
- Leaders concentrate on setting direction and ground rules, and establishing individual roles.

Storming:

- The reality of what needs to happen and when hits home. People get really busy.
- Cliques can start to form, conflicts arise, power struggles emerge and personal agendas surface.
- Authority, ways of working and tasks may be questioned while others jockey to be in the good books with the leader.
- Leaders spend their time listening, coaching and building up levels of teamwork.

Norming:

- Resistance and differences are overcome.
- Cohesiveness develops – people start to appreciate individual team members' strengths, ask each other for feedback, and share more of themselves and their opinions more readily.
- Individual agendas are set aside for group goals, and confidence grows.
- Leaders challenge the team to avoid groupthink and start to include them in bigger picture decisions.
- This doesn't mean everything is smooth sailing – there may be times when new tasks arise and the team slips back into Storming, but they can rebound back to Norming sooner.

Performing:

- Structure is set and works well for the team. Roles become flexible and functional.
- Members' confidence is high and channelled to the task, and they can work with minimal supervision.
- Members share praise and constructive criticism productively.
- Leaders spend their energy delegating, developing team members and aligning activity to emerging trends.
- Not all teams get here – it all depends on how they manage conflict.

Adjourning:

- Some teams reach this naturally (think of a project with a beginning and end date), while others not so naturally (think restructure or a significant number of members changing teams in a short period of time).

- It is important for this stage to be acknowledged – the work and results achieved up to this point.
- The team needs to realise change is required and to move on from the previous ways of doing things. What worked here may not work in the future.

Tuckman's model of team development is still referenced and relevant today when it comes to identifying how teams work together and progress.

As good as Tuckman's model is, however, I am not sure if we have progressed that much in terms of how well we work together. In Australia, 91% of workers' compensation claims that involved a mental health condition were linked to work-related stress or mental stress, and 58% of those claims were due to work-related harassment, bullying and pressure.[17] In Canada, it's not much better. Nearly half (47%) of working Canadians agree that their "work and place of work is the most stressful part of their day and life".[18] I am not sure of similar statistics from the 1960s, however my instinct tells me they wouldn't have been much worse or better. According to Fierce Inc's 2011 study of 1,400 corporate executives, employees and educators, 99.1% prefer a workplace where people identify and discuss issues truthfully and effectively, yet only half of those said their organisations do so.

Norwegian adventurer Thor Heyerdahl once said, "Progress is man's ability to complicate simplicity." If this is the real definition of progress, then maybe we are doing a good job when it comes to working together. It seems working together is getting more complicated.

So what's the answer to working better together, or to doing 'together' better? How do we get teams to swear by each other and not about each other? To swear in front of each other and not behind each other's backs?

If you believe in Dr Google, a search for 'characteristics of high performing teams' will provide you with around 53 million answers. Boom, perfect. With such an abundance of information available, leading a higher performing team should be as easy as putting together an IKEA bookshelf, right?

Wishful thinking.

Let's go back to Tuckman's model. I wonder if Forming, Storming, Norming, Performing and Adjourning do still apply in today's world. I am certain you could look at any of the definitions of the stages and place your team in one or two of them.

Where things may have changed is the pace at which teams need to move through these stages.

For example, imagine you are the CEO of a sporting event and you had less than 18 months to create a team of up to 60 people (plus over 1,000 volunteers) to deliver an event on a global scale. This was the case for Nick Hockley, CEO of the organising committee for the ICC T20 World Cup of Cricket in 2020. Nick and his team were responsible for delivering one of the biggest sporting events ever staged in the Southern Hemisphere.

Can you imagine Nick and his team taking:

- 3–4 months to get through the Forming stage
- Another 6–8 months to get through the Storming phase, and
- A couple more months to transition into Norming ... and then hopefully by the end of the year, Performing?

Bloody hell – I suspect if it took this team 12–14 months to get to the Performing stage, there wouldn't be any beer available to buy at the stadiums. No beer. Imagine the furore. The event would be over. Stadiums closed.

Why we need to change the time frames and be deliberate about team development

Think about how consumer and employee expectations have changed. Their patience is lower and they're not quite as forgiving as they once were. Consider:

- 47% of consumers expect a webpage to load in 2 seconds or less; 40% abandon a website if it takes more than 3 seconds to load.[19]
- A 2013 study analysed an unprecedented 6.7 million unique viewers from around the world who in aggregate watched 23 million videos for 216 million minutes. The study discovered that online videos begin losing viewers at a delay of 2 seconds, and every 1 second of waiting after that marks a 5.8% increase in the number of people who leave.[20]

Seconds people, we are talking seconds! This means we need to be much more efficient in delivering videos as well as working together in the workplace. In your case, it may not be seconds but it may not be far off. Email/text/WhatsApp/pick your weapon (or poison), communication often necessitates a response within hours, sometimes minutes. 'Necessitates' may be debatable, but in some cases it's true.

So where is your team at? If it's not in the Performing stage, then you have a couple of options. One – you can wait and hope for nature to take its course and for the team to (hopefully) get there on its own. Or two – you can take deliberate steps to help improve how your team develops as a group. You can accelerate the pace at which you create cohesiveness and work towards swearing by each other. And it can all start now.

Key Takeaways

☑ There are many models to help identify how teams work together, spearheaded by Bruce Tuckman's classic model of team development. You could also check out Rubin, Plovnick and Fry's GRPI Model of Team Effectiveness, Katzenbach and Smith's Team Effectiveness Model, Lombardo and Eichinger's T7 Model of Team Effectiveness, and Hackman's Model of Team Effectiveness, as well as LaFasto and Larson's book *The Five Dynamics of Team Work and Collaboration*, and Lencioni's work *The Five Dysfunctions of a Team*.

☑ Working out how to manage conflict is key to moving from Storming to Norming to Performing.

☑ Some teams need to move through the stages more quickly than others. Therefore, you will need to put deliberate focus on the key activities of each stage.

Reflections

💡 Think about your team. On a scale of 0–10, with 10 being at its fullest potential and 0 being the opposite, what score would you give your team?

💡 What is interfering with your team reaching its potential? Once you answer this question, ask yourself, 'What else?'

💡 What else? And what else?

CHAPTER 2

What the research tells us

Scott Dinsdale is a pretty interesting guy. Born in Kingston, Ontario, Canada, Scott at one stage was the head of global distribution and CTO for Sony Music, after which he led Accenture's Media and Entertainment business across Asia. He is now the Managing Director of Future Next, a digital advisory and business development service across media, entertainment, sports, finance and retail.

Not only is Scott's resume pretty impressive, you need to see his hair. He would give Michael Bolton a good run with his long, cool locks. On top of a good lid, Scott's passion growing up was music, and he even tutored a couple of the members of the Tragically Hip. The Hip was a band that was absolutely revered by Canadians. To give you an idea of what they meant to the country, Canada's Prime Minister Justin Trudeau delivered the national eulogy at the passing of their lead singer. Anyways, I digress. Scott and I were discussing the Tuckman model and he suggested, similar to Tuckman, that it takes time for teams, whether in music or business, to operate at a high performing level. If the board or executives expect big results right away, they are going to be disappointed. And Scott is not alone in thinking this. Former Wallabies player and co-founder of GainLine Analytics Ben Darwin also suggests for a team to succeed, they need to be a cohesive unit, and that builds over time through shared experiences.

Building cohesion does take time. Look at music bands. Some of the world's greatest rock bands rose to the top after spending a ridiculous amount of time together. Some even started playing together when they were in high school. Members of Radiohead, Rush, Green Day and INXS have played together since high school. Mick Jagger and Keith Richards went to primary school together.[21] Four of the five members of the Tragically Hip grew up in the same town and two went to school together, which is where their collaborations started. Perhaps one of the most famous stories about music, time and cohesion is The Beatles. They are renowned for having played over 10,000 hours together before they hit the big time in North America.*

Does more time together help teams perform better and therefore work more productively? In a leadership survey, McKinsey Consulting reported 72% of 191 organisations said team performance has an impact on productivity.[22] I think it's fair to say time helps people connect, build trust and get a better understanding of how each other works. For many of us, we don't have 10,000 hours (which is roughly 5 years of Monday to Friday work) to become a high performing team. Often, we don't have 8–12 months as some would suggest is required to get through the different stages of team performance.

So what is the key to becoming a high performing team? Regardless of how much Japanese Roku gin a team drinks at an offsite, it (probably) won't happen overnight. What I've tried to do for the rest of this book is share with you what I've found makes a difference. I believe—as others do—if you deliberately and consistently focus on what makes a higher performing team, you

---

* Malcolm Gladwell's *Tipping Point* goes into much more detail about this. I highly recommend reading this book.

can generate better results. And in a radically quicker time frame than if you let things just 'naturally' occur.

The Wu-Tang Clan and the Russian hockey team

In 2017, McKinsey reported that, "Every year, more than 10,000 business books are published, and that's before you add in hundreds of thousands of articles, blogs and video lectures."[23] I'd suggest a fair amount of those 10,000 business books touch on characteristics of high performing teams. Patrick Lencioni's *The Five Dysfunctions of a Team* is an oldie but a goldie. Shane Snow's *Dream Teams* is also really valuable, particularly because it references the 1972 Russian ice hockey team and one of the greatest rap bands ever, the Wu-Tang Clan, as two high performing teams. The 1972 Russians and the Wu-Tang Clan? A match made in heaven. We will touch on some of the tactics used by the Wu-Tang Clan in Chapter 17.

If you are a left-brained research and numbers type of person, many studies have been conducted around the world on what makes teams work better together. Google's Project Aristotle looked at 180 teams across their business. When they analysed the differences between the teams that performed better versus those that didn't, five traits—in order of importance—stood out:

1. **Psychological safety** – Team members felt safe to take risks and be vulnerable in front of each other. This was the most important trait in Google's study.
2. **Dependability** – Team members got things done on time and met Google's high bar for excellence.
3. **Structure and clarity** – Team members had clear roles, plans and goals.

4. **Meaning** – Work was personally important to team members. They were working on what they cared about.
5. **Impact** – Team members thought their work mattered and created change. All team members felt their team was making a difference.

We will go into much more depth about psychological safety in Chapter 15, however its importance within teams cannot be understated. Psychological safety helps develop trust and respect in teams and allows team members to admit mistakes and ask for help. I suspect those working in the Australian banking sector could have used a little of this prior to the Royal Commission into Misconduct in the Banking, Superannuation and Financial Services Industry. Again, more about that later.

'It's how you teach the game'

This was the slogan for Ajarty Sports Consulting, the first company I started, alongside baseball guru Sheldon 'Artie' Sawatzky.* We were hell-bent on helping well-intentioned parents, who were typically full-time workers with little experience in their children's sport, to become better youth sport coaches. We ran clinics for parent coaches and created a resource to support them. Our main message was for parents to avoid getting too hung up on teaching the technical components of skills and to focus more on running an effective practice that included a lot of movement, fun and energy. Teaching the technical components to young children was as difficult to teach as it was to

---

* 'Artie' is short for Arthur Murray, as in the school of dance. Apparently, Sheldon was such a smooth dancer in his heyday, he was given the nickname to recognise his moves, and the name has stuck ever since.

learn. Try teaching a child who has never picked up a baseball and ask them to throw it overhand—one of the most unnatural movements ever—let alone trying to break it down into step-by-step instructions. So our main message was not to worry so much about *what* the parent coaches taught, but to focus more on *how* they taught the game.

It turns out we were onto something.

The Massachusetts Institute of Technology (MIT) has undertaken several fascinating studies into human interaction. One in particular highlights that it's not necessarily *who* you hire that will drive success, but more *how* your chosen hire communicates with other team members. It's how they communicate, not necessarily who communicates.

Professor Alex 'Sandy' Pentland, a computer scientist who directs the MIT Connection Science and Human Dynamics labs, is one of the most cited scientists in the world. In 2011, Forbes declared him one of the "seven most powerful data scientists in the world".[24] You know who topped him that year? Google's CEO. And the CTO of the United States Department of Health and Human Services. A pretty impressive crew to be associated with.

In 2012, Pentland released an article entitled 'The New Science of Building Great Teams', in which he shares a number of learnings he developed while working with 2,500 people from 21 organisations across a variety of industries. Being a data-capturing guru, he literally put his wares to work. By asking participants to wear sensors and wireless technology, Pentland was able to observe how people in teams engaged, with the aim of being able to predict which teams would succeed or fail based on how team members interacted. As Pentland stated, the technology captured "more than 100 data points a minute and work[ed] unobtrusively enough that we're confident we're capturing natural behavior".

One of the biggest surprises was the impact on team success of "individual reasoning and talent". Pentland's research suggests these two factors contribute far less to team success than one might expect. "The best way to build a great team is not to select individuals for their smarts or accomplishments," he noted, "but to learn how they communicate and to shape and guide the team so that it follows successful communication patterns."

Pentland was as surprised as everyone else with some of the results. As he commented, "It seems almost absurd that *how* we communicate could be so much more important to success than *what* we communicate."

Pentland's five key findings into what characterises higher performing teams were as follows:

Finding #1

The best predictors of productivity were a team's energy and engagement outside formal meetings. He credited these two factors with a third of the variations in dollar productivity among groups.[25] When working with a call centre in a bank, by simply encouraging teams to take their breaks together instead of one person at a time, Pentland found that the average handling time (an important KPI in call centres) improved by more than 20% among lower performing teams. Apparently, the call centre manager changed the break schedule at all 10 of the bank's call centres and forecasted US$15 million a year in productivity increases. That's right, US$15 million a year. This move also saw employee satisfaction improve by up to 10%.[26] Not bad.

Finding #2

Similar to the advice my mentor Miles Callaghan gave me, Pentland found when everyone on the team talks (shares their opinion) and listens in roughly equal amounts, teams perform better. Note that it's not 'everyone is given the opportunity' to contribute – they actually contribute. Verbally. The key is to keep contributions short and sweet. The task for leaders then becomes finding ways to ensure everyone contributes. And keeping those contributions short and sweet. Pentland also found that when members carry on back-channel or side conversations within the team—even in meetings—they perform better. Although it might sound counterintuitive, the findings demonstrated that at times, more than one person speaking doesn't hurt teams.

Finding #3

Pentland found that the best way for teams to communicate was face-to-face, facing one another, with conversations and gestures he characterises as 'energetic'. Get this – his research showed that "35% of the variation in a team's performance can be accounted for by the number of face-to-face exchanges among team members". Yes, 35%! Far out. Simply by speaking face-to-face, with a little care factor. Serial emailers – this is your time to run and hide behind a rock. Pentland found that texts, emails and instant messages were the least effective forms of communication. Videoconferencing can be effective but as the number of people increases, the effectiveness of the meeting goes down.

Finding #4

Teams whose members connect directly with one another—and not just with the team leader—perform better.

Finding #5

Pentland's research demonstrated that where team members periodically break—go exploring outside the team and bring information back—perform better. Carly Loder, who at the time of her appointment was one of Australia's youngest chief marketing officers, has noted that her team has applied this approach on several occasions. While developing Kayo, the 'Netflix of sport', Loder and her team would occasionally consult globally with similar service providers outside of the sports ecosystem. As she described to me:

> Because we were working on something that had never been done before (in the sporting landscape), there was no precedence, no internal learnings or experience we could leverage. So we started looking outside to see who else was doing this in a different industry and luckily we found one in the UK. It saved us time and a lot of fumbling around, all through a couple of conversations.

So what's the magic formula?

Similar to Google's algorithm for getting yourself onto page one of the search results, there is no single answer for creating teams that swear by each other. Pentland's approach is one of many. All these numerous studies and approaches, however, do start to point us in the right direction, and a number of common characteristics start to emerge for creating the foundations of higher functioning, higher performing teams. What if we could combine all these characteristics into one, simple model? A checklist to refer to when things are not going so well? Or even better when things are going well and could be even greater? Hmm, if only such a checklist was available. The good news is there is such a thing. Soon, you'll find out.

Key Takeaways

☑ *The Five Dysfunctions of a Team* and *Dream Teams* are great resources to inspire higher performing teams. Recent research from Google and MIT also provide useful insights.

☑ Psychological safety has been proven to be a key factor in higher performing teams. It is fundamental to learning from one another's experiences, developing trust and avoiding the same mistakes over and over.

☑ How teams communicate is more important than getting the best talent on a team.

Reflections

🔅 What form of communication does your team rely on the most? Ask your team and see what they say.

🔅 In your team meetings, whose voices are heard most of the time? Whose are not?

🔅 Based on Pentland's five findings, what's one step you could take to help your team increase the chances of more swearing by each other rather than about each other?

CHAPTER 3

The two foundations of high performing teams

Establishing a higher performing team requires a focussed leader who truly believes in people and has the courage to stand up for what they believe in. How many organisations say, 'Our people are our number one asset', and then when times get tough (or targets aren't hit), what gets cut? Training. Development. Offsites. Travel budgets. People. At least it's good to see some senior executives still investing in connecting over fine wines at some of the top restaurants in the country. I am a big believer in connecting, but whether a bottle of Dom Perignon from the Illuminator at Vue de Monde (one of Melbourne's finest restaurants) is necessary is another issue.

In Oliver Stone's 1999 hit movie *Any Given Sunday*, Al Pacino delivers one of the most stirring speeches to his team before they take the field for "the biggest battle of our professional lives". With great passion, he implores them to fight for every inch of the field.

On this team, we fight for that inch. On this team, we tear ourselves, and everyone around us to pieces for that inch. We claw with our fingernails for that inch. 'Cause we know when we add up all those inches that's going to make the f*cking difference between WINNING and LOSING, between LIVING and DYING.

When it comes to working with sporting teams, the metaphor of inches is a good one, and it's just as applicable in the workplace. The question becomes which inches do you claw with your fingernails for when it comes to developing your team? What makes higher performing teams swear by each other instead of about each other?

And where is this bloody checklist I mentioned earlier? Well – let's get into it.

In my experience, depending on the level of clarity and relationships, teams across all sectors—whether they be in the corporate, sporting, education, movies or music settings—can sink, spin, self-serve, or best of all: shine.

Clarity and relationships. The two foundations upon which higher performing teams are built.

I have developed a team dynamics matrix to help leaders nail down what they need to focus on to get their teams shining. Is the team's clarity low? What about the quality of their relationships? By exploring the different quadrants in my team dynamics matrix we can figure out how to get our teams shining. Because really, who wants to be spinning, self-serving or sinking?

Table 2: The AB Team Dynamics Matrix

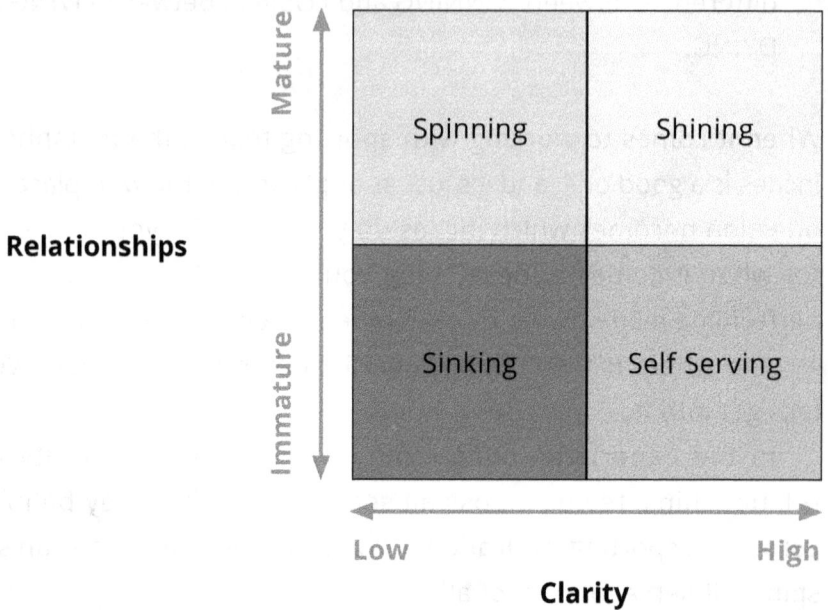

Teams that are *sinking* are typically struggling and achieving little if any success. We will explore the characteristics of sinking teams in Chapter 6.

Teams that are *self-serving* are characterised by erratic performance. They are made up of some winners, some losers, and often some sinners. We'll go into more detail about self-serving teams in Chapter 7.

Teams that are *spinning* are characterised by people who work well together yet make little meaningful progress. We'll learn more about these teams in Chapter 8.

Teams that are *shining* are made up of team members who are all winning, influencing across the business and making a big difference. Chapter 9 will delve into shining teams.

Let's now dive deeper into the first foundation of higher performing teams, clarity.

CHAPTER 4

Foundation #1 – Clarity

On 11 December 1998, NASA's Mars Climate Orbiter was launched into space. The satellite, which came with a hefty price tag at the time of US$125 million, was supposed to be the first weather observer used on another planet. Ten months later, on 23 September 1999, the project hit a speed bump. Or a star. Or something. The orbiter disappeared. The highly anticipated probe was scheduled to begin orbiting Mars that morning. However, around 5:30am NASA officials lost communication with the satellite. Scientists realised quickly it was gone for good.

"It was pretty clear that morning, within half an hour, that the spacecraft had more or less hit the top of the atmosphere and burned up," recalled NASA engineer Richard Cook, who was project manager for Mars exploration projects at the time.

So what happened? A NASA review board found that the problem was in the software controlling the orbiter's thrusters. The software calculated the force the thrusters needed to exert in pounds of force. A separate piece of software took in the data assuming it was in the metric unit: newtons. Lockheed Martin, the firm that built the orbiter, used the imperial form of measurement, while NASA used the metric. No one realised this, however, until it was too late.[27]

How did this happen?

According to folklore, a Lockheed Martin engineer confirmed with a NASA engineer, "We are measuring things in metric, right?" And the reply given was, "Yes". However, what the Lockheed engineer didn't hear was one of the assistants asking the NASA engineer at the same time, "Would you like a coffee?" Apparently the 'yes' was in response to the coffee. Not the confirmation of which measurement system to use.

Doh!

Whether this explanation is true or not, I don't know. What I do know is that a lack of clarity ended up costing NASA a lot of wasted time and money and created a huge amount of stress for those involved. The reality is that a lack of clarity can do the same for you and your team.

Dealing with ambiguity

In 2018, LinkedIn Learning surveyed 2,968 professionals and asked them what the most frustrating quality they had experienced in a manager. The runaway winner was "a manager whose expectations aren't clear or frequently change". Creating clarity around expectations typically begins with the leader, then the ongoing conversations within the team keep the clarity a consistent force. If a manager is not creating clarity for their team— say, for example, not creating clear goals and objectives—it's probably because they themselves are not clear. When I was leading a marketing team, one of our goals was to lift brand engagement. Outside of quarterly customer surveys, we didn't have any measurements in place. I struggled to articulate which inputs we could measure to drive the outcome. My boss also struggled to articulate this. As a result, I'm not sure I put my team in the best position to succeed. I suppose the saving grace was our lack of clarity didn't cost us US$125 million. Rocker Billy Joel once said, "I am, as I've said, merely competent. But in an age of incompetence, that makes me extraordinary." By creating clarity, you too can be extraordinary.

Let's avoid bashing the boss's incompetence though (or rather my incompetence at the time!). When it comes to teams and tasks, there is always going to be some level of ambiguity. And priorities will change. In the world of online streaming, priorities can change in as little as 15 minutes. As Carly Loder from Kayo described to me, she needed to adjust to making decisions every 15 minutes based on customer data as it came through:

There were other sporting programs we were streaming on a weekend which we anticipated would be more popular. Leading up to the weekend, we had a number of marketing materials ready to use for the other sports and very little for The US Masters. We were very clear on our approach and it all got thrown out of the window quickly. We had to change our approach very quickly that weekend – which meant a couple of nights working until 11pm. It was frustrating but that's the world we live in now.

It was frustrating but that's the world we live in now.

With this ever-changing world, senior management might often suggest the more we can deal with ambiguity, the more successful we'll be. I agree with this. Well, sort of.

I believe leaders sometimes use the line 'deal with ambiguity' as a result of not having all the information available to make a decision. There are times when it's critical to deal with ambiguity – look at how the world had to deal with COVID-19. Very few could plan for that. However, where possible—even if it's hard—the clearer leaders can be, the better their teams will do.

Best-selling author Steve Maraboli wrote, "It's a lack of clarity that creates chaos and frustration. Those emotions are poison to any living goal." Chaos, frustrations and poisons are usually not the best for teams. Although navigating ambiguity is an important skill, creating clarity is an even more important one.

When it comes to creating clarity within a team, there are four main areas that are critical for building alignment. When you get these right, oh boy, that's when some magic can happen. You can be nimble and quick. You can make shit happen instead of shit happening. These four areas are:

1. Team purpose
2. Objectives
3. Roles and responsibilities
4. Team behaviours

1. **Clarity on team purpose.** The compass that gives you direction. The rudder on the boat. The North Star. The glue that binds a team together and makes a team a team. Whatever metaphor tickles your fancy, the clearer everyone is on the purpose of the *team*, the easier it will be to make decisions, to say yes or no to opportunities, and to do great stuff. If the team is not aligned on the *team* purpose, it's like a team of rowers pulling out of sync. Frustrating. Painful (to watch and be part of). And not fun. If everyone is pulling together, it might still be challenging, but it's so much smoother and more satisfying.

2. **Clarity on objectives.** According to leaderchat.org, 57% of managers see misalignment during goal cascading as a big challenge. In the same report, 44% of employees, while familiar with company goals, could not specifically name them. Far out, that drives me nuts. Imagine going into work every day and not having anything specific to work towards. How would you know if you are achieving anything worthwhile? How would you track your impact, and understand if you were making a difference?

3. **Clarity on roles and responsibilities.** When it comes to creating clarity in this space, it's all about how to best manage the grey. Getting agreement on being flexible early on also helps. Typically, job descriptions include lists of bullet points outlining what a person is responsible for. The challenge with job descriptions is that they are created in a moment of time, based on what is happening right then and reflecting what the hiring manager needs at that point. In the real world though, things change very quickly. Another challenge is that the bigger your organisation gets, the harder it is to know what's happening everywhere. Even in smaller teams, which may have clarity on their objectives, there can still be an overlap of responsibilities with other teams. We also interpret things differently, so what we think a job description covers may not be the same as what the next person thinks. This can cause issues. The sooner team members are clear on what needs to be done, who will contribute and how they will do it, the sooner the team will get shit done instead of getting shitty. And they'll swear less about each other too.

4. **Clarity on team behaviours.** There's a saying in golf that you can drive for show and putt for dough. At work, I like to say you can talk for show and do for dough. Your beliefs don't

27

make you a better person, your actions do. And for every team, there will be a set of behaviours that will make the difference between winning and losing. The sooner a team can identify those behaviours, agree how to make them part of their ways of working and what to do if they are not followed, the better the team will be.

We will have a closer look at creating clarity across these four areas in Chapters 10–13, and I'll share key insights into what you can do to create greater clarity across your team.

CHAPTER 5

Foundation #2 – Relationships

When it comes to human needs, there are few theories as popular as Abraham Maslow's Hierarchy of Needs. First published in 1943, Maslow's paper 'A Theory of Human Motivation' suggested humans have five basic needs. The model suggests that individuals must satisfy lower-level deficiency needs before progressing on to meet higher-level growth needs.[28]

Table 3: Maslow's Hierarchy of Needs

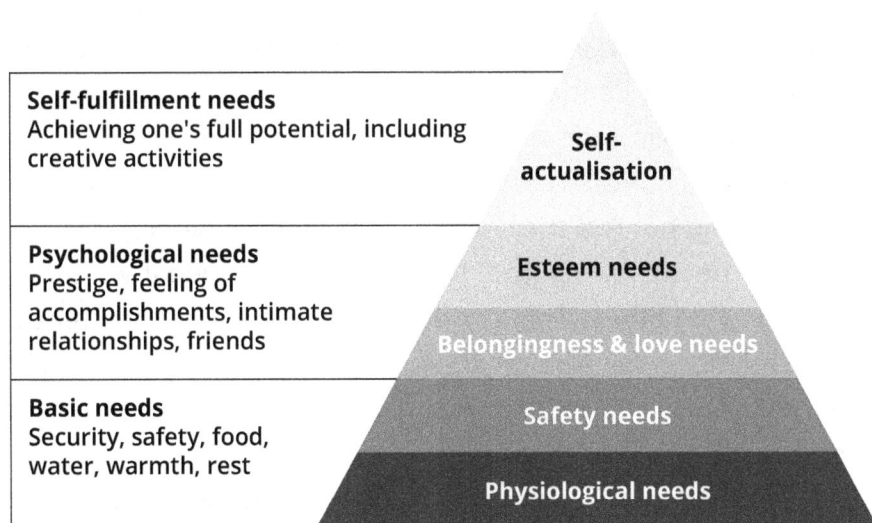

Self-fulfillment needs Achieving one's full potential, including creative activities	Self-actualisation
Psychological needs Prestige, feeling of accomplishments, intimate relationships, friends	Esteem needs
	Belongingness & love needs
Basic needs Security, safety, food, water, warmth, rest	Safety needs
	Physiological needs

When we think about individuals and work, we could assume that the first need falls under the responsibility of the individual. When we look at the next level of individual needs—safety, belongingness and love—these rely on relationships. When we are talking about teams, relationships are critical. Jon Talebreza-May, an Assistant Professor of Social Work at Pacific University, confirms this: "The value of 'the importance of human relationships' is the foundation upon which everything else is built."[29] Unless, as Aristotle suggested, you are a god or beast: "Man is by nature a social animal. Anyone who either cannot lead the common life or is so self-sufficient as not to need to, and therefore does not partake of society, is either a beast or a god."

So when it comes to working together, what do relationships look like? Does enjoying a nice drop of red wine after work together constitute a good relationship? What about keeping each other up to date with the latest gossip? Or organising (or attending?) a morning tea? While there are elements in these activities that can help people bond, there's more to developing strong working relationships than organising cupcakes and balloons for someone's birthday. As Alex Pentland from MIT has demonstrated, strong relationships do include a social element. But strong relationships also mean we connect, create an environment where we can drop our guard and not feel the need to simply nod to be nice. We can shake our heads for 'no' too. Ideally we can say what we think, sooner, and ask others what they think, without feeling threatened. Strong relationships also mean we can disagree, like the Wright brothers often did, to get the best outcome (more about the Wright brothers later).

As outlined in an Australian Workplace Psychological Safety study, 81% of workers are not working at optimum levels. *Harvard*

Business Review reported that 58% of employees trust strangers more than their boss. And *CFO* magazine reported that 70% of mergers fail to achieve their anticipated synergies, while 50% suffer an overall drop off in productivity in the first 4–8 months.

And the reason why?

Because we don't recognise the human factor is the most important factor. Clinical psychologists Shoba Sreenivasan and Linda E Weinberger note that, "Humans, because of necessity, evolved into social beings. Dependence on and cooperation with each other enhanced our ability to survive under harsh environmental circumstances."[30] Growing up in Canada, we learned about how First Nations people travelled together, often in groups of 400. Together, tribes would build teepees and pit houses to survive the long, cold and harsh winters. They hunted animals and gathered plants for both food and medicinal purposes. And they would protect each other from other tribes and hostile animals (wolves look pretty nasty to me!). Essentially, if these groups didn't work together, they wouldn't survive. Nowadays, even though the threats to our physical survival may have reduced, we continue to have a need to affiliate with others.

So what are the keys to mature relationships at work?

Based on my research and experiences, there are four characteristics of mature relationships at work:

1. Connection and trust
2. Psychological safety
3. Feedback
4. Conflict

1. **Connection and trust.** Joe Maddon, the manager of the 2016 Chicago Cubs who led the club to their first World Series in 108 years, repeatedly said that without connection, you can't have trust. "With my players, we built connection first, and after a period of time, we started trusting each other. If you don't nurture the connection followed by trust, you will never arrive at a free exchange of ideas, without someone getting upset because you don't agree with them. That's the only way you get the best out of the group."

2. **Psychological safety.** This term was coined by Dr Amy Edmondson, an American scholar and Novartis Professor of Leadership and Management at Harvard Business School. Edmondson defines psychological safety as a shared belief that the team is safe for interpersonal risk taking. This means people can be themselves and express their thoughts, disagreements and mistakes without being afraid of negative consequences. As mentioned in Chapter 2, Google's Project Aristotle identified psychological safety as the top characteristic of their highest performing teams.

3. **Feedback.** Is it seen as insight or criticism? Robert Allen, one of the most influential investment advisors of all time, said "There is no failure. Only feedback." What a great mindset. According to the Convergence International Snapshot of the Australian Workforce, only 47% of workers receive praise or recognition for work well done. And the *Harvard Business Review* has reported that 57% of survey participants stated they prefer corrective feedback rather than praise. Unfortunately, our brain initially sees feedback as a threat, and our body's response is the same as it was in prehistoric times when we were threatened: fight or flight. The good thing is that feedback in the workplace doesn't

result in loss of limbs like threats our ancestors faced. In high performing teams, feedback is encouraged; it is sought regularly and given in the right way.

4. **Conflict.** Is conflict seen as a sign of respect and encouraged? Or is it avoided and only used to raise the blood pressure? Conflict is simply a disagreement amongst people and can be extremely productive when it's handled the right way – in the Inner Sanctum of Conflict. But it can also be characterised by antagonism and hostility, hallmarks of the Outer Sanctum of Conflict. Conflict handled in the Outer Sanctum is like tits on a bull – bloody useless. We'll visit the Inner and Outer Sanctums of Conflict later in Chapter 17.

We will look at these four areas in more depth in Chapters 14–17 to help you and your team create stronger relationships. You'll be swearing by each other instead of about each other in no time.

Key Takeaways

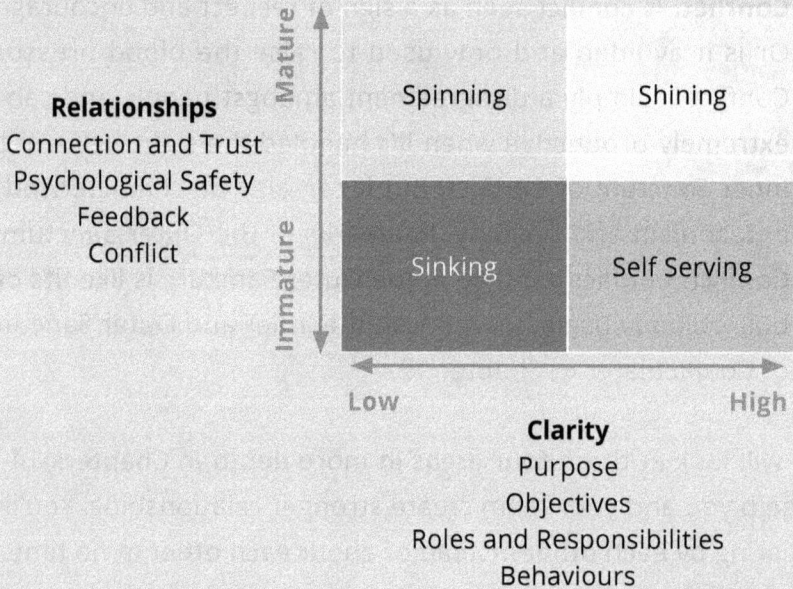

Relationships
Connection and Trust
Psychological Safety
Feedback
Conflict

	Low	High
Mature	Spinning	Shining
Immature	Sinking	Self Serving

Mature → Immature (vertical axis)

Clarity
Purpose
Objectives
Roles and Responsibilities
Behaviours

☑ Having clarity on team purpose, objectives, roles and responsibilities, and team behaviours is vital for creating a higher performing team.

☑ Mature relationships at work rely on connection and trust, psychological safety, sharing feedback, and a productive use of conflict.

☑ Creating clarity and strong relationships requires a constant and deliberate focus by the leader and the team. Get these things right and your team will shine – I swear!

Reflection

- When looking at the four areas of clarity, where is your team 100% aligned? Where is it not 100%? What do you think that is costing in terms of real dollars?
- When looking at the four areas of relationships within your team, what does your team do well?
- If there was one thing your team could do to get closer to the shining quadrant—as far up and to the right as possible—what might it be?

SECTION 2

Diagnosing Your Team

Now that we know what we mean by clarity and relationships, let's have a look at the four types of teams where clarity and relationships are present and absent. As we explore sinking, spinning, self-serving and shining teams, have a think about which one sounds like your team. You may find some of the characteristics sound familiar ... great! By diagnosing where your team is today, you can use the learnings from this book, as well as your own intuition and experience, to determine what you can do to move your team closer to shining. Ready? Right on, let's go.

CHAPTER 6

Is your team sinking?

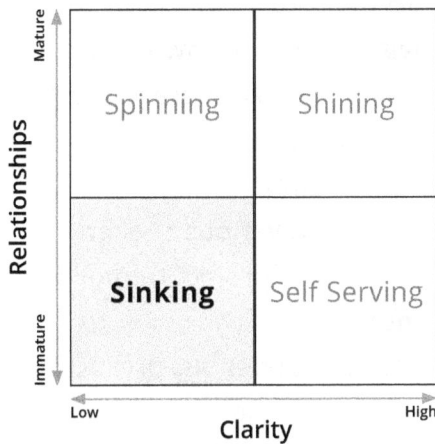

Relationships — Mature / Immature

	Low ——— Clarity ——— High
Mature	Spinning	Shining
Immature	**Sinking**	Self Serving

One day I received a call from a former colleague of mine, Heidi Clarris. Heidi is very switched on. She's got a PhD in Neuroscience with undergraduate degrees in both science and psychology. She's also one of the most level-headed people I know and is the calming force when situations get heated. Heidi has spent a good chunk of her career in leadership roles in social policy, consumer research and health services across the corporate, not-for-profit and government sectors. She was promoted to a high-profile role at Bupa, tasked with bringing together some of Bupa's best experience managers to create signature experiences for Bupa insurance, aged care, optical and dental customers as well as Bupa's 22,000+ employees across New Zealand and Australia. The role was highly contested, and Heidi was the chosen one.

Heidi quickly recruited six internal team members, a mix of researchers, customer experience designers and project managers. All very capable people with a diverse range of backgrounds, styles and approaches. The team was located across Melbourne and Sydney.

Two months into the role, Heidi called me. She explained that the team was struggling, and her own levels of frustrations were mounting. While it sounded like there was a good level of mutual respect within the team, she said cracks were starting to show. Progress was stalling on projects. She was starting to hear from some team members about various challenges working with each other. One person wanted a project to move much more quickly. Another felt they needed to slow down to ensure all risks were identified. Whilst this was happening, pressure was mounting from senior executives to deliver. The team was slowly sinking.

As Heidi shared: "I really needed the team to start sorting out their issues. I didn't have the time to be playing moderator, and to be honest, I was finding it really draining to come to work. It is not the team dynamic that I wanted to foster and I needed to do something to change."

The team was very polite in front of each other. There was a lot of nodding to be nice yet a lack of confidence to disagree and take risks in front of each other.

To be fair to the team, the challenge they had all signed up to was a big one. They were trying to do something the organisation had never done before. They were attempting to work across three business lines, thousands of people and multiple departments, and determine how to consistently design and deliver signature experiences. All of this at a time when customer experience design was in its infancy in Australia, and not well understood by senior leaders. When you combine all this uncertainty and weaker relationships you end up with a team that is sinking.

Have you seen the movie *Shawshank Redemption* with Morgan Freeman and Timothy Robbins? In 1947, banker Andy Dufresne (Robbins) is convicted and sentenced to two life sentences for the murder of his wife and her lover, and sent to Shawshank State Penitentiary in Portland, Maine to serve his time. At one point in the story, Andy is sent to solitary confinement. When the guards come to release him from solitary, they open the heavy door to his cell and find him curled up in a ball. He is beaten, he is alone, and he is not well in the mind. This is what it can feel like for a team that is sinking.

Heidi's team wasn't at the bottom of the pit, but they were close; they were displaying a number of the characteristics of a sinking team:

- A heavy reliance on the leader to solve all problems
- Very few people, if any, are winning
- Engagement declines – people start wondering what their next job will be
- People's energy levels are drained because they feel like they are on their own
- Decisions take a long time to make; when they are made not everyone supports them
- Issues amongst team members are not raised and remain unresolved
- Disagreements are not shared

- Creativity is stalled
- Work is done – but little is delivered
- Swearing about others sometime happens. Worse yet, over time, swearing at oneself starts to take place. Self-doubt takes over. Stress and mental health issues may start to arise

A number of these characteristics were showing up in Heidi's team. Team members felt they were not delivering any value and started asking themselves what they were doing there. Issues were being shared with Heidi but not resolved amongst team members. Individuals had to dig deep for energy as the days went by. Deliverables were few and far between and decisions were taking a long time to be made. Team members were frustrated and didn't feel comfortable working out disagreements amongst themselves.

The great thing about Heidi is that she recognised the team was sinking and did something about it. We kicked off our engagement with an AB Team Dynamics Baseline Assessment, which is a diagnostic tool I have created to help leaders assess the strength of relationships and levels of clarity across their team. The assessment outlines positive and negative aspects of a team's dynamics, as well as (my favourite) team dynamic blind spots. The assessment and facilitated discussion unlock actionable insights to improve how teams work together. Once I shared the assessment results with Heidi's team, we were able to identify opportunities to improve the quality of the relationships and create higher levels of clarity about what the team could control.

I remember looking at my watch during the team dynamics assessment review, thinking we needed to move along. I looked at Heidi and she signalled to me to keep the discussion going.

As Heidi recalled: "During the session, we were able to get to a depth of conversation that had not been possible before. I had been trying to get the team to have this conversation for weeks, so it was critical for them to keep talking. It created the most open conversation the team had had at that stage."

You could sense the feeling of relief as the team shared their concerns and frustrations. The energy lifted, people were swearing in front of each other and the team was making progress. They connected. They were creating a safer environment to take risks and disagree – in front of each other! And they agreed these new behaviours needed to continue. Together, we were able to identify a number of key behaviours that were critical to this team's success, including:

- Saying things sooner
- Accepting a captain's call when needed and backing that decision once the call had been made (whether they agreed with it or not)
- Ensuring each person's wellbeing was looked after
- 'Rule #6'* – not taking themselves too seriously

As a result, the connections grew stronger across the team. A few months later, Heidi shared her observations:

Are we a high performing team? Not yet. We still have some work to do with the broader business about clarifying a few things. Are we a higher performing team? Are we better off? Absolutely. Since the session, we have been more open and honest with each other than ever before which has already created more confidence and trust to say what we think and move forward.

---

* Curious about this? Check out *The Art of Possibility* by Benjamin and Rosamund Zander.

Heidi wasn't the only one who thought so. We conducted a follow-up AB Team Dynamics Assessment to measure the progress of the team and compared the results to the baseline report. We also surveyed the team to get a feel for how well the new team behaviours were becoming embedded. We identified that the time to make decisions had halved. Issues were being brought up—get this—20 times more quickly! 20 times! Simply by 'saying it sooner'.

As Heidi said: "We make decisions with less time going around and around. Our efficiency as a team has improved noticeably, and we talk much more honestly with each other."

Key Takeaways

☑ Grudges, blame, avoidance, absenteeism and tiredness are all signs the team could be sinking. Team members on their mobile phones in the parking lot is another sign that things may not be great.

☑ It's important to get the team to share their perspectives as soon as possible. Creating a safe environment for team members to share is important. Gathering qualitative data or engaging an external facilitator can help unearth difficult situations and provide a framework to talk through any issues in a productive manner.

☑ As a leader or team member, you have a duty of care. If you notice signs of mental health issues starting to appear, it's important to seek expert advice.

Reflections

💡 Think about when you've been sinking at work – what impact did it have on you at home?

💡 Looking back on that time, what advice would you give yourself, knowing what you know now?

💡 What are the signs you need to keep an eye out for to stop your team from sinking?

CHAPTER 7

Is your team self-serving?

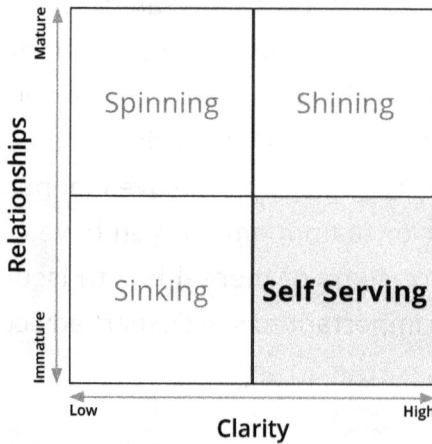

Like many Aussie actors, Heath Ledger could attribute his kickstart as an actor to one of Australia's longest-running dramas, *Home and Away*. Ledger appeared in 10 episodes as bad boy Scott Irwin who took advantage of the lovely Sally and broke into Principal Fisher's office to steal copies of an upcoming exam. Eventually, Sally exposes Scott's devious acts and he is expelled. After which Ledger moved on to bigger and better things.

Years later, Ledger played the Joker, the central villain in Christopher Nolan's *The Dark Knight*. An anarchistic mastermind, the

Joker schemes to undermine Batman's influence and turn Gotham City upside down with erratic and chaotic behaviours.

Perhaps Ledger's initial role on *Home and Away* was good preparation for his future depiction of the Joker. Lies, deceit and questionable behaviours were defining characteristics of the Joker. In an interview with *The New York Times*, Ledger described *The Dark Knight*'s Joker as a "psychopathic, evil, schizophrenic clown with zero empathy".

The Joker embodies what it's like to work in a team that is self-serving. Self-serving teams have high levels of clarity of what they want to achieve. But they have poor, shallow relationships. This results in short-term success for some and ongoing struggles for others. Over time, performance declines.

Self-serving teams typically have the following characteristics:

- Some winners and some losers, and at times sinners and losers
- Engagement and performance vary, as does mental health
- Less delegation occurs so burnout is a real risk for some
- Energy is often expended on the wrong kinds of activities, such as undermining and throwing people under the bus
- The 'no dickhead' policy does not apply
- Over time, feelings of guilt, resentment, hurt and indifference for each other build up
- Gossip is rife. If people are swearing, they are swearing about each other and typically behind each other's backs
- While all team members might be working towards a common goal, people feel like they are working on islands. Collaboration is typically forced rather than encouraged

Sales teams are sometimes characterised as self-serving teams. A group of individuals, doing their own thing to hit their targets. This isn't always the case, as one of best shining teams I worked on was a sales team. However, in the example below, I was definitely part of a self-serving team.

When I was appointed as a regional sales manager of retail stores selling financial services products, I was quite excited. This was my first time managing managers, a critical skill identified by a great mentor of mine, Eric Granger. Eric spent over 30 years in sales management so when he spoke, I listened.

In our state team, there were four regional sales managers (RSMs. Each of us looked after a set of retail outlets within a geographic area and led 25 to 35 people, including store managers and sales consultants.

My new team (my peers and manager) had a variety of skills, backgrounds and experiences. One of the RSMs had been in their role for six months, joining the team from a similar role and industry with another organisation. Another RSM had been in her role for a couple of years and was a great teammate and star performer. A third RSM started on the same day I started, moving over from a different industry. And me – I had been with the company for more than five years. Not long after we started, a new state manager was also appointed who had been with the company for a few years in a B2B sales management role. Our team assistant had been in the same role for over five years.

Co-founders of operations and management consultancy GainLine Analytics, Ben Darwin and Simon Strachan (whom I have run Leadership Performance Labs with) would suggest our team had a low level of cohesion. GainLine has created algorithms to predict team success in sport and business. They look at how a person's previous experience can affect individual and team performance. And by experience, they mean experience with people, their positions (that is, their roles) and their programs (or systems and processes). This research suggests external experience doesn't always act as a positive.

This makes sense. External recruits typically bring in processes and systems that worked for them in their previous environment. When these processes clash with the existing processes in their new environment, external recruits spend valuable time proving their systems are better while existing team members spend valuable time protecting their current systems. Once the new processes are (finally) agreed upon, more chaos ensues as they are rolled out to the broader team. As Ben says, "Teams spend more time working out what processes to use and implementing them instead of focusing on things that matter. In most cases, it doesn't matter if you create the perfect new process or have the 'best' system. The key is for teams to work together in a cohesive manner on what matters most."

Predictably, our team of regional sales managers experienced a period of chaos. One RSM continued to strive. Another came in and hit the ground running, applying their experiences and (new) processes from previous roles to their region. Another RSM's performance was starting to drop. Me – I struggled. Externally, I held my own, just. I listened to my store managers, made a couple of tweaks here and there, dealt with a couple of people issues and saw a quick lift in performance. Over time though I was battling inside. I didn't know how to deal with the high number of people-resourcing challenges that came with retail. Luckily, I had a couple of peers from other states I trusted that I could share my challenges with. Throughout the week, they received numerous 'WTF' calls from me. At home, my wife had to deal with a husband who at times was a mess and struggled to sleep over the stress.

In terms of clarity, our team had a clear purpose and objective: we were to drive sales and service standards as per the sales targets. Our roles were clear and we spent time identifying the behaviours necessary to succeed.

Like most self-serving teams, where performance is unstable and inconsistent, we were talking (and at times swearing) about each other behind each other's backs. As a regional sales leadership group we rarely leveraged the whole team's knowledge and best practices. Some team members would make broad statements that were rarely backed up with any action. This resulted in a lot of eye-rolling from the rest of the team, followed by a lack of trust. Questionable behaviours began to appear, which became a real distraction for our team. Yet none of us addressed any of these issues head on. 'That's not my job' was the prevailing attitude.

Our leader had a big challenge ahead of him. He had a team full of ambitious individuals, some who knew what they were doing, some who thought they knew what they were doing and some who didn't have the experience yet to know what to do (the last one being me).

In our first year, our state achieved its target but not all centres or regions did. Within 12 months, two regional sales managers had resigned (that's 40% of the leadership team). There was a lot of gossip. It was a difficult situation for our state manager, and over time he had to manage a number of tricky situations. As a group, we dropped the ball in leaving this to our manager to navigate on his own.

So why didn't I do anything or say anything? Good question. I know why I didn't. I was frustrated. I felt hard done by some of my fellow RSMs because they didn't appear to be that helpful. I remember sitting in team meetings and hearing about initiatives from one of my colleagues thinking, 'Why didn't you share this with all of us earlier, we could have all done this!' Over time, my frustrations grew and I became resentful. I was talking about others behind their backs and not providing any kind of feedback. I avoided conflict. I wanted out. I still remember some of those sick stomach feelings. It was exactly a year to the day that I started in the regional sales manager role that I accepted another role in a different department.

Looking back on it, as clear as we were on our purpose, objectives, roles and behaviours, the lack of strong relationships within our team let us down. I lacked the courage and skills to have challenging discussions with some of my colleagues. I didn't ask for help from everyone – I didn't want some of them to realise I was struggling. And disagreements amongst the team were rarely voiced in front of each other – but I certainly know they were voiced behind each other's backs.

As SJ Watson, author of *Before I Go to Sleep*, says, "It's so difficult, isn't it? To see what's going on when you're in the absolute middle of something? It's only with hindsight we can see things for what they are." In hindsight my time as an RSM was beneficial to me in a number of ways. Most importantly it was where I learned the value—or rather the price—of keeping the guards up, of not having challenging discussions, and of letting the ego rule the roost. As a result, our team's performance was inconsistent, it spiked up and down, as did my own. Not ideal. A very self-serving team.

Key Takeaways

☑ Self-serving teams have some winners, some losers and some sinners.

☑ Poor relationships in teams lead to higher levels of turnover, a lack of honesty and higher levels of stress.

☑ Showing vulnerability, calling out poor behaviours, and making feedback part of the conversation can help move teams from self-serving to shining.

Reflections

💡 Who could you ask for ideas about good activities to strengthen the connections within your team?

💡 Looking across your team – who is not performing at the level you'd like them to be? What role might the team—or you—be playing in this?

💡 Who might you need to ask for help that you've been avoiding?

CHAPTER 8

Is your team spinning?

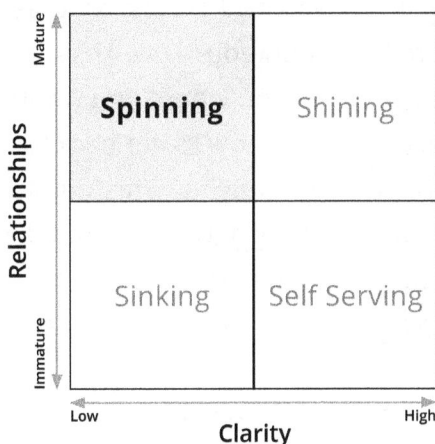

Spinning	Shining	
Sinking	Self Serving	

Relationships (Mature / Immature) vs *Clarity* (Low / High)

Growing up in Saskatchewan, long cold winters were the norm. Three feet of snow was a permanent fixture by November. Throughout the winter, we could get anywhere from 10 millimetres to a metre of snow at a time. Mix in some warm weather (the odd day we would get over 0 degrees Celsius) and a few weeks of –30s and –40s (yes minus, and that's Celsius), it made for some challenging driving conditions. Getting stuck, sliding out of control and trudging through the ruts were common occurrences when driving on the roads in the Paris of the prairies.

I can remember one time as a child when we were at the Esquirols' house for dinner. They were family friends who lived on a farm in the North West region of Saskatchewan, about an hour from the closest city. When you're in the farming regions of Saskatchewan, all you can see are flat prairie fields. They say it's so flat in Saskatchewan you could sit on your front porch and watch your dog run away for three days.

On the evening we left the Esquirols' house it had been snowing for a few hours. There was no lighting on these country roads, no road signs to help you on your way. Essentially you relied on your local knowledge to get you where you wanted to go. Dad had grown up in the area so knew how to get back to my grandparents' farmhouse, where we were staying. This night was a little more challenging. I remember sitting in the back-middle seat of our 1983 Oldsmobile Delta 88, with my two younger brothers, eyes glued to the road, hoping that our car would not veer off into the ditch.

Then we got stuck.

Dad was going back and forth between drive and reverse, trying to gain traction, straining to get that big four-door sedan moving one way or the other. Forward backward, forward backward. We weren't making any progress. If anything, we were making deeper ruts, digging ourselves a deeper hole. We got out and pushed and pushed and pushed, but to no avail. I can't imagine the stress my parents were experiencing. Midnight, three children under the age of 10, and stuck in the middle of Timbuktu in freezing temperatures. I can remember Dad rugging up—grabbing his gloves, toque and an extra jacket—and venturing off into the black night which seemed like oblivion, en route to a local farmer's yard a few kilometres away. Desperate times called for desperate measures. After what seemed like an eternity, partly because of the worry we had for

Dad and partly because you can only listen to Neil Diamond's 'Hot August Night' cassette for so long, I can still remember seeing the headlights of a tractor with a plough on the front approaching us. Dad had made it and a rescue was on the way.

Working in a team with strong relationships but a lack of clarity can be like our Oldsmobile Delta 88 that night. You get stuck. You spin your tyres – whether it's in the snow, the mud or in the office.

It was like a proposition development team in the financial services industry I was engaged by. The team had a high level of direction from their department's management. It was quite a generic direction but in theory, could impact business across two countries and multiple P&Ls.

The team put considerable time and effort into developing their relationships. They could disagree productively and call each other on behaviours if they didn't align with the team's way of working together.

However, they did not achieve success.

The team's tasks crossed over with other teams' tasks and deliverables. Over two years, the team worked extremely hard, but because there hadn't been agreement on what their purpose was in the big picture of the business, and how success would be measured, predictably they had a hard time gaining any traction and buy-in from the other departments. The team got to the point where they couldn't tell if they were making any progress, which caused frustrations to mount – within their team and with other teams.

Unfortunately, this team was not as fortunate as we were on that cold, dark night in Saskatchewan. Despite their strong relationships, the team's lack of clarity and agreement on what success looked like *across the business* ultimately resulted in a lack of meaningful progress or return on investment.

The team was disbanded and roles were made redundant. Some team members questioned whether the work they undertook over two years was worth it. It seemed they had been spinning their tyres without making any real progress.

Spinning teams get along really well and feel comfortable challenging each other but in the end, make little meaningful progress. This is because they often lack alignment on the big-ticket items like purpose, objectives, roles and responsibilities, as well as key behaviours.

Warning signs your team might be spinning and struggling for clarity include:

- A lot of time and energy is put into making a difference – with very little tangible evidence of any progress happening. As a result, energy and engagement drops
- A few of the people in the team succeed ... hopefully
- Resentment starts to build for some, as the focus becomes about individual progress instead of team progress; others remain oblivious and just keep working harder and harder
- Duplication of effort drives inefficiencies, resulting in a low ROI
- The swearing that occurs is usually about other parts of the business ('They don't frickin' get us!'). But ultimately, when there is a lack of clarity, it typically falls on the shoulders of the leader – who is then also on the receiving end of plenty of swearing

Key Takeaways

☑ Just because your team is getting along doesn't mean they are making meaningful progress. Ensure all team members are clear and aligned with the key elements of what you're trying to achieve and what it's going to take to do it.

☑ Ensure you regularly review your team's purpose, objectives, roles and responsibilities, and behaviours. Business context can change quickly, and your team needs to adapt.

☑ Over time, teams that are spinning teams often result in resentment, resignations or sometimes – redundancies. The good news is the key actions to helping your team move forward—discussion and decisions—are within your control.

Reflection

🔆 When have you been in a team that was spinning? What did you learn from that situation that you've applied from that experience?

🔆 Out of team purpose, objectives, roles and responsibilities, and team behaviours, which one do you think your team is most aligned on? Why do you think this is?

🔆 How might you be contributing to a lack of clarity across your team?

CHAPTER 9

Is your team shining?

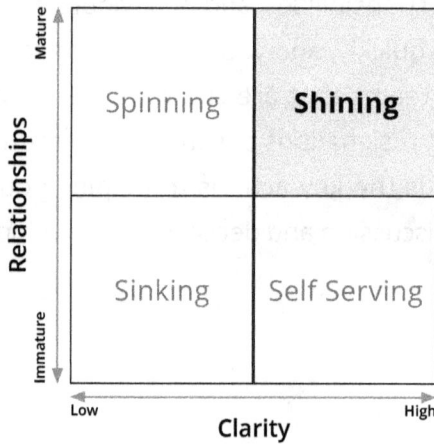

At the end of the movie *Shawshank Redemption* (warning, spoiler alert), our friends Andy Dufresne and Red reunite on a beautiful beach in Zihuatanejo, Mexico. After his escape from prison, Andy cashes up, withdraws the Prison Warden's laundered money from several banks and begins his new life. Red is eventually released on parole and struggles to adapt to life outside of prison until he meets up with Andy on a sunny beach in Mexico. Andy is sanding down a boat and looks up to see his good friend walking toward him. It's a heartwarming scene, signifying the end of years of struggle and the start of something new. The music playing during the scene is melodramatic and triumphant; if it were set in the present day, Imagine Dragon's 'On Top of the World' would be a suitably upbeat choice.

Think of when you worked in a high performing team. What song would characterise how you felt? Did your team have a high level of clarity and deep relationships? No wonder it was shining.

Teams that are shining typically share the following characteristics:

- Success is achieved by the team and by all individuals
- Engagement and commitment to the team and business are high
- Everyone contributes, works hard and energy is renewed
- Team members—for the most part—enjoy each other's company. There may be some rough patches, but team members work through them and move on
- And of course, everyone is swearing *by* each other

Imagine you're going for an interview for a role in an existing team and the person interviewing you describes the team like this:

- High achievers – all team members have overachieved on their sales targets and received significant bonuses
- Half of the team's members have been recognised as the top performing national representatives at a sales conference in Cancun
- The leader of the team has been recognised as manager of the year
- The team works well together, they have disagreements and don't always do the right thing. But they bring those issues up, deal with them and move on
- They are often held as the gold standard for teamwork

Whilst there might not have been a boat waiting for this team like there was for Red, the description above is of a team of pharmaceutical reps who cast aside the typical stereotypes of a sales team to drive outstanding results and create pretty special relationships.

Non-sales folk typically see sales representatives as focussed on one thing and one thing only, and that's hitting their personal sales targets. In 2004, I was fortunate to have been part of a team where we all achieved something pretty special, and it was one of the best experiences of my professional and personal life.

Of the team of six, four of us were working with GPs and two others were working with specialists. We each had a hierarchy of products we focussed on. For example, the main medication I promoted was Diovan (a blood pressure medication), my secondary focus was Elidel (a treatment for eczema), and Famvir, a treatment for shingles, cold sores and genital herpes,* was third on my list. For my teammates, Tim's priorities were Diovan #1, Famvir #2 and then Elidel as #3. Trent and Michelle also promoted similar medications with a different weighting of importance. Adrienna worked with physicians who specialised in cardiology, and Jeremy worked with psychiatry specialists. Prior to this, Jeremy had worked with the GP reps promoting the same product lines we were now promoting so he had a good knowledge of our products and customers.

---

* On a side note, putting aside the seriousness of the medical conditions, I must admit I found the herpes medication quite humorous to promote. I kid you not, at one stage the genital herpes sales aids compared a clean-skinned banana to a bruised banana to show the differences between a treated 'banana' and an untreated 'banana'.

As this was only my second 'real job' out of university, I didn't give much thought about our team dynamics. Upon reflection, I realised there were a number of factors working in our favour:

- Our individual objectives and incentives were set up so that it was beneficial to work together. If the organisation had only assigned one product to each of us, human nature could have kicked in and we would have naturally focussed on only promoting our one product, thereby missing the true value of collaboration.
- Our leader Liz was very supportive. She was a great teacher who gave and sought performance feedback.
- Face time (not the phone app, rather spending time together in person) was prioritised. Throughout the week, we were on the road or working from home so we didn't naturally see each other that often. However, Monday morning coffee meetings at the Bagel Shop on 8th Street were prioritised for everyone. Without fail. We would share who we were visiting that week, get insights from previous visits and plan initiatives together. We'd also hear a new dad joke from Tim. This forum provided us with a way to connect on a regular basis and ensure everyone was on the same page about who was doing what.
- There was very little ego across those in our team. The group was motivated and supportive. As the new guy on the team, they made me feel like I could ask anything and not be frowned upon from day one. No one was competing against anyone else to stand out more than others. And one of the best team players of all was Jeremy, who was always there sharing his knowledge and time even though he had a completely different portfolio of products than the rest of us.

- It wasn't always smooth sailing. I remember a few challenging discussions across the team – in team settings and one-to-one. They weren't a regular occurrence, but a few spread out over the year that either cleared up some misunderstood actions or were reminders for the group about what we needed to focus on.
- What made this team special was not only how we did things, or what we achieved, but what we got out of it in the bigger picture. We became friends. Just like the outcomes of the MIT research, we had regular social interactions. We'd catch up as a group along with our partners on a Friday afternoon/evening at someone's house to prepare goody bags for an upcoming conference. We'd have each other over for barbecues. We played on a beach volleyball team together. When it came to Christmas parties, we'd go for dinner and then end up at someone's house to play card games and laugh at Tim's dad jokes. My wife and I spent a lot of time with Jeremy and his wife while we lived in Canada. When retired athletes talk about what they miss the most about playing on a team, they often talk about the friendships. Whilst we weren't professional athletes, I felt the same.

At the risk of sounding high and mighty, our team kicked ass. The team and individual results were some of the best in the country. Three members of the team were recognised nationally. Our leader Liz was recognised as Manager of the Year. Team members won quarterly national competitions.

Now this sounds all hunky-dory doesn't it? Or it might sound unrealistic. The reality is, it isn't unrealistic. It can be done. You've seen it before, you've been a part of it before. That doesn't mean it's easy. It does take hard work. Working in a team that is shining comes with its fair share of struggles and challenges. We are humans, we make mistakes and at times, we respond in peculiar ways. But by deliberately focussing on creating strong relationships and high levels of clarity, you can make a difference. You can make a meaningful difference. And heck, you can even have fun and make new friends while you're doing it.

So what are the signs that your team is shining?

- People enjoy their work and at times are more than happy to give discretionary effort.
- You hear 'I disagree' or 'Here are my thoughts' and people respond with 'Tell me more'.
- People work hard, at times are tired, but find ways to renew their energy.
- The team learns and takes on stretch assignments.
- The team has influence more broadly across the business.
- When personality clashes arise, the team sorts shit out themselves.
- The team looks out for each other and looks for ways to help each other out.
- The team swears by each other, and not about each other.

Key Takeaways

☑ Teams that focus specifically on creating clarity amongst themselves and making their relationships stronger typically outperform as a group, and outperform as individuals.

☑ Teams that are shining don't always get along, but they can work through disagreements together and make meaningful progress.

☑ Shining teams often create a deeper connection than just work, allowing team members to get more out of work than just a pay cheque.

Reflections

🔆 Think about a time when you were in a team that was shining. If you were being interviewed by *Harvard Business Review*, what would you say made the team 'shine'?

🔆 What challenges did the team face? How did you collectively overcome them?

🔆 What's one thing you could contribute to your team now that would help make it shine?

🔆 This brings us to the end of Section 2 of *Teams that Swear*. Now that we have explored the Team Dynamics matrix and gained an understanding of the different types of teams, have a think about where your team sits in the matrix. If your team is already shining, the next section could reinforce what you need to keep focussing on. If your team isn't shining yet, it's now time to look at how you can make it shine by focussing on clarity and relationships.

SECTION 3

How to Create Higher Performing
Teams with Clarity

Author Brené Brown has a great phrase, "Clear is kind. Unclear is unkind." When it comes to working in teams, this is especially true. When we're thinking about creating clarity, remember that sharing is caring. Clarity is based on shared knowledge, and shared knowledge comes from sharing information regularly and openly, allowing people to make and buy into decisions based on what you know at that moment in time.

Over the next four chapters, we will explore the key areas you need to create clarity in, and how to do it in the workplace, to move your team toward shining. Whilst sharing the company strategy, setting company targets, establishing job descriptions and making sure everyone knows how to get things done is a start, it is not the finish. It is the finish if that's all you do. Unfortunately, it's the finish of meaningful progress. To keep moving forward and making meaningful progress, you need to create and maintain clarity.

CHAPTER 10

Creating clarity with purpose

Purpose is deep, resonant and permeates an environment to create a sense of identification and connection that is so powerful— you would do almost anything to partake. It's a reason for being that inspires and lights you up from the inside. Purpose is an expression of the contribution we wish to make in order to help the world become a better place.
~ Author Stephen Scott Johnson

The purpose of an organisation, of a team and of a leader acts like a guiding light and becomes the key filter for ideas and decisions. Organisations who get it right and do it authentically drive higher levels of engagement, effort, creativity, teamwork and customer focus. In this chapter we will review the importance of purpose for an organisation, for teams and for leaders, explore how to identify your team's purpose, and figure out how to ensure everyone is clear and on the same page.

In his book *The Purpose Economy*, author Aaron Hurst shares the story of Dolf van den Brink's arrival in the CEO role of Heineken USA. The business had not been performing well, internal conflict was holding it back and it was clear it needed a turnaround. Looking back at the origins of the 150-year-old, family-controlled company, van den Brink discovered that in the early 20th century, Heineken was known for its "very progressive labor policies, offering savings and loans and healthcare to its employees, and taking care of the communities we operated in".[31] He took this to his team and asked, "If we were doing this in the early 20th century, why can't we do it today?" As a result, the company put in place new policies, including paternity and maternity leave, and flexible benefits, and worked to ensured work-life balance. Van den Brink credits this act of digging back into the company's original leadership purpose as a contributor to an "impressive business turnaround, restoring top line growth and consistent market share gains".

This story is a great example of how purpose can make an impact on business. It is becoming increasingly apparent how important it is for businesses to articulate their purpose. In their report 'Business Case for Purpose', Ernst & Young partnered up with Harvard Business Review Analytic Services to understand the importance of purpose for an organisation. The report concluded: "Those companies able to harness the power of purpose to drive performance and profitability enjoy a distinct competitive advantage. Laden with many meanings, the core insight about this notion of 'purpose' is that meaning matters—not just in an abstract sense, but in terms of today's business metrics."[32] The report also highlighted that businesses that prioritised articulating their purpose experienced 10% growth year on year over the past three years, noticeably better than those organisations that were still articulating their purpose and better again than those that had not yet started to think about or articulate their purpose. The study also revealed that executives believed a "strong sense of collective purpose drives employee satisfaction", can help "increase customer loyalty" and can "affect an organization's ability to transform".

Look at companies like IKEA, who wants "to create a better everyday life for the many people".* Or Lego, which exists to "inspire and develop the builders of tomorrow", which, they explain, means "to inspire and develop children to think creatively, reason systematically and release their potential to shape their own future – experiencing the endless human possibility". Or Interface, one of the world's largest manufacturers of modular carpet for commercial and residential applications. Although not as sexy as Lego or IKEA, their purpose is to "lead the industry to love the world". This may be a curious statement for those not familiar with the company, but since 1994 Interface has aimed to sell carpet without having a negative impact on the environment, accepting years of losses in the spirit of doing the right thing—loving the world—from an environmental and social perspective. Interface is a fantastic example of a business using their purpose to help drive a bigger impact across the globe.

What else do these companies have in common?

- They all have a greater purpose than making a profit. Most want to do good because they realise the impact they can have that goes beyond the bottom line. They can help make something better. This type of purpose motivates teams. It helps us all achieve some portion of our 'self-actualisation'. Interface even proves that you don't have to make profit all the time to achieve your purpose.

---

* Some may debate whether going to IKEA, let alone putting IKEA furniture together, is fun but it is an organisation that has an inspiring purpose and resonates with millions around the world.

- The purpose will attract people who are passionate about that specific purpose. This means recruitment, retention and effort levels will most likely be better. Not everyone likes kids, so Lego may not be for everyone. But IKEA's practical, far-reaching vision is something most people can get behind.
- The purposes are short, sweet and simple, and easy to remember. A seven-year-old could—and should—be able to understand it.

Personal purpose

Purpose is not exclusive to organisations. Personal and team purpose are just as critical.

When it comes to personal purpose, people often look for purpose through their work. In a survey by Convergence International, addressed to full-time, part-time and self-employed individuals, 72% of Australians said they were looking for purpose and meaning through their work. Many business schools across the world take their students—top business leaders from around the globe—through a combination of self-reflection, coaching and exploration exercises to help them find their leadership purpose. Once they are clear on their purpose, they can use it to not only lead with authenticity, but also as a guide for many of the big decisions they will make.

Our mate Dolf van den Brink from Heineken also had his own leadership purpose: "To be the wuxia master who saves the kingdom."[33] Nick Craig from *Harvard Business Review* worked with Dolf to help him come up with this, reflecting Dolf's "love of Chinese kung fu movies, the inspiration he takes from the wise, skillful warriors in them, and the realization that he, too, revels in high-risk situations that compel him to take action".

Completing the Trifecta of Purpose – Your team's purpose

When it comes to articulating and aligning on purposes that impact work, it is just as important to have clarity on the team's purpose as being clear on the organisation's and your own leadership purpose. Without team purpose, teams try to do too much and their to-do lists become cluttered. This results in a constriction of the impact they can make.

In an ideal world, an individual's purpose will align perfectly with their organisation's purpose, which then allows for the team's purpose to contribute to both the organisation's objectives and the individual's. This is the Trifecta of Purpose and is a win-win-win situation. When the trifecta is *completed*, discretionary effort increases. Innovation and growth are enabled. Teams are focussed. And everyone has a personal interest in making meaningful progress.

However, if one of the three purposes is not clear and aligned, watch out.

Table 4: The Trifecta of Purpose

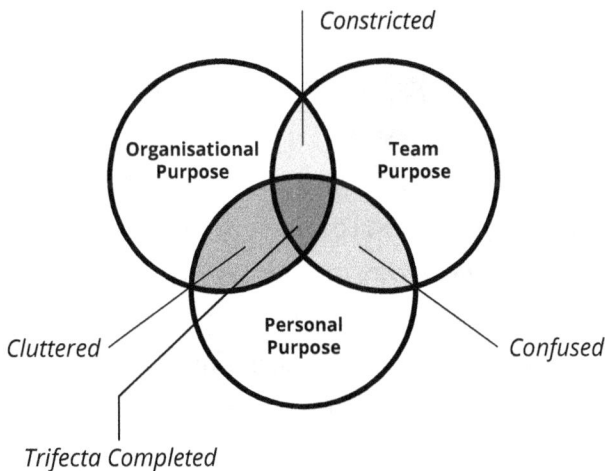

When the team's purpose is not aligned with the personal and organisational purpose, you will often find the team's agenda to be *cluttered*. Personal ambitions can make it hard to maintain the right focus, there is often duplication of efforts between various teams and the to-do list becomes very long. Over time this becomes overwhelming for the team and its members and can lead to unproductive interdepartmental conflict.

When one's personal purpose does not align with the organisation's and team's purposes, the outputs for the team are *constricted*. An individual's efforts and energy are shared or limited and sometimes torn between what they do at work and what they want to be doing with their lives. Little innovation occurs, getting the minimum job done is the norm and this misalignment reduces the impact one can make at work and more broadly.

When personal and team purposes are not aligned to the organisation's purpose, you run the risk of creating *confusion*. Personal and team preferences drive priorities and decisions, which can cause confusion and a lack of meaningful progress for individuals in the team, other teams and eventually for customers.

Establishing clarity on your team's purpose

Creating your team's purpose gives team members a clear sense of what their own contribution to the company means and how they can approach their work day in and day out.

According to a 2018 *Forbes* article, for teams, having a "grander purpose isn't about tapping into some mystical internal drive but rather about creating simple beacons that focus attention on a shared goal".[34] Research suggests team members will actually revert to pursuing their own selfish interests in the absence of a team connection powered by purpose. This 'shared intention' is an indispensable and essential component of teamwork.

Whilst a company's purpose is critical to set the direction and ambitions of the company as a whole, each team's contribution is where the real passion can be ignited, because this is where personal impacts are made. The team's purpose answers the question, 'How do *we* make an impact?' and by extension provides direction for 'How do *I* make an impact?'

Having a team purpose shares all the benefits of a company purpose, with the extra benefit of often making up for personality clashes within teams. Retail investment specialist Douglas Isles from Platinum Asset Management shared this sentiment on Matt Battye's podcast, *Choices*, pointing out that "having the right motivation to perform together can be more important than whether you like each other".

So does it make sense for teams within an organisation to have a different purpose than the organisation itself? Absolutely. As long as the team purpose is aligned with the broader purpose of the company. Whilst IKEA's IT department contributes to creating a better everyday life for the many people, how specifically do they do that? What is going to inspire the IT testing team to contribute to the broader purpose? You guessed it, the team purpose.

Two other great models for identifying purpose are Simon Sinek's The Golden Circle, which works well for companies and teams; and filmmaker, producer and author Adam Leipzig (former Disney executive who supervised such films as *Dead Poets Society* and *Honey, I Shrunk the Kids*) who has a great exercise called 'How to Know Your Life Purpose in 5 Minutes'. These models simplify the process of finding your team's purpose (and your own) and serve as a basis for meaningful discussion amongst your team. Check them out.

Developing a team purpose case study

As a global health and care company, Bupa's purpose is to help people live longer, healthier, happier lives. This purpose is one of the organisation's greatest strengths. It is a draw card when recruiting. And once you join the organisation, the purpose inspires passion across many of their 22,000+ employees. Working with Bupa's Insights and Net Promoter Score team in Australia reinforced this for me.

The Insights team was led by Simon Gaymer, a senior manager whose team's employee net promoter score was consistently amongst the top echelons of Bupa's global leaders. This pretty much meant that people who worked in Simon's team loved working at Bupa and with Simon.

Whilst many of the 22,0000+ loved working at Bupa, not everyone did. So what made Simon's team different? As he noted: "I like to back up the organisation's talk about people being a priority by focusing on team development and dynamics. And by that I mean, taking the time to reflect as a team, are we doing the things we are good at, are we providing value to the business and our customers, and are we doing it in a way that gets us excited?"

Simon's commitment to this reflection was more than talk, demonstrated by engaging me to work with his team. I asked him why, with his team's employee net promoter score so high, did he see the need to bring in an outside consultant to work with his team? Things seemed to be going pretty well. Perhaps typical of someone who has worked in the insurance industry for a number of years, his response was related to risk management. Simon shared:

> I see these types of activities like an insurance policy. You can assume things are going well, but by doing something like this allows the team to confirm we are in a good place, or realise we could be

in a better place. I find issues are brought up in these forums that are not shared in our regular routines throughout the year.

The second reason is because I talk a lot about the importance of prioritising team development and as easy it is to say "we're too busy" or "the budgets are too tight this year", I believe these things need to be backed up with action on my end, and Bupa's end. Hence why we are doing this.

Part of my time with Simon's team involved reviewing and creating alignment on the team's purpose. The group asked themselves, 'How do we contribute to helping people live longer, healthier, happier lives?', with their specific strengths, skill sets and what they were passionate about. To help them, I took them through Adam Leipzig's 'How to Know Your Life Purpose in 5 Minutes' exercise (check out his TEDx talk of the same name). The exercise works equally well for individuals and teams. To find their team's purpose, Simon's staff answered the following five questions. I've included the team's responses so you can see how it all comes together.

1. **Who are you (your name or your team's name)?** Bupa's Insights and NPS team
2. **What do you do (what does your team do, keep it real simple)?** Listen to Bupa's customers and tell their stories
3. **Who do you do it for (who are your customers)?** Our (internal) business partners
4. **What do they need or want?** To connect and understand their customers
5. **How do they (your customers) change or transform as a result of what you do?** Deliver value and drive continuous improvement

Once you've answered these questions, it's like putting a puzzle together. All you have to do is answer question 5, then questions 1 through 4.

Putting it all together, it sounds like this:

(Question 5) The Insights and NPS Team exists to help Bupa make decisions that deliver customer value and drive continuous improvement. We (question 1) do this by listening to Bupa's customers and telling their stories to connect (question 2) our business partners (question 3) to their needs (question 4).

As a group of researchers, they were passionate about uncovering and delivering insights to help make a difference. And their purpose summed up that passion succinctly. Their team purpose, like your team purpose:

- Makes no mention of making money. Or about being the best. It's about helping the organisation's purpose
- Can attract the right people. Researchers are typically curious to help make some sort of sense of something, like exploring (listening in this case) and enabling change
- Acts as a good filter for what they should be focussing on and how. Helping drive customer value, listening to customers and sharing their customer stories. Very clear. Throughout the year, the team did just this. One initiative of particular interest was their customer showcase, an expo-type event where they shared various customers' stories and insights with departments across the business
- Was articulated in a way a seven-year-old could understand the team's purpose

A few months later, Simon commented that there were two benefits in having the team come up with the purpose. One – the team's buy-in to the purpose was strong. This is what they came up with and believed in, and it ensured their work aligned with their purpose. And two – it allowed the team to differentiate themselves, and clearly explain what they did and the value they brought to the business.

The bottom line is that we all need something to stand on and stand for. Something that makes us fight for something bigger and better. No matter how large or small your job, getting clear on how you and your team contribute to the larger story will help drive meaningful progress. And a team purpose will help you do that.

Key Takeaways

☑ Businesses with a stated purpose, and that take the time to ensure their employees understand it, have the ability to perform better, achieve higher levels of engagement and make bigger impacts.

☑ A team's purpose is just as important as the organisation's purpose so that team can connect to the bigger purpose and understand the impact they make.

☑ Review the team's purpose regularly to ensure everyone remains clear and aligned to what motivates them to continue making a difference, for the business, the team and each individual.

Reflections

🔆 What is your team's purpose? Ask your team the same question. Instead of getting them to answer the question out loud, ask them to write it down first then share it. Compare your answers.

🔆 When you decided to take on your current role, what attracted you to the company? What attracted you to the role? What were you hoping to achieve? On a scale of 0–10, how close are you to achieving your purpose?

🔆 When was the last time you shared your answers to these questions with your team? How could sharing them help?

CHAPTER 11

Creating clarity with objectives

In 1979, a group of MBA graduates from Harvard were asked about their goal setting habits. The results were very interesting:

- 84% of the graduates did not have goals
- 13% had a plan in mind but did not write their goals down
- A mere 3% had goals that were written down

Ten years later, they revisited those interviewed about their goal setting habits. And guess what? The 13% who had goals were 10 times more successful than those who didn't have goals and earned on average twice as much as the 84% who didn't have any goals. And the 3% who had goals and had written them down? They were earning 10 times as much as the other 97% put together.[35] A similar study in 1953 at Yale University demonstrated similar results.

Funnily enough, there is conjecture as to whether these studies actually occurred. From my research I could not find any of them. So this made me think – is having goals and writing them down actually beneficial? Why even mention these studies if their existence is questionable?

Well, here's my view. Talking about making meaningful progress is one thing. And making it happen is another. Objectives help us direct our attention mentally and behaviourally toward what really matters. They also give us a way to measure progress. Without them, it's very easy for us to get distracted and spend our energy on tasks that don't contribute to our broader purpose.[36]

Throughout this chapter I will refer to objectives and goals interchangeably. I know some see them differently, however my view is we can make things complicated when we don't have to. So, throughout this chapter, I refer to objectives (and goals) as the end outcome an individual or group of people is trying to achieve.

Transparency with your objectives

With clear objectives, you and your team can understand the kind of impact you are making and whether or not you are making progress that matters. If you want your team to make progress that matters, there are two key steps when using objectives:

1. Set them
2. Share them

This seems ridiculously straightforward; however, I have seen far too many examples of teams and individuals struggling to set objectives for the year or for a specific piece of work. Despite our best intentions, how many of us end up finalising our annual objectives three months ... or even further ... into the year? I have also experienced a reluctance for teams and individuals to share their team or individual objectives, leading to an overlap of work, missed opportunities and a waste of time, money and talent.

By setting clear individual and team objectives and ensuring teams share their objectives with each other, groups can work smarter, minimise duplication of effort and expenditure, and put themselves in a better position to create better outcomes.

Frameworks for setting objectives

Articulating team and individual objectives is important for creating clarity amongst teams. Two common frameworks include SMART objectives and Objective and Key Results, better known as OKRs.

SMART objectives

The SMART objectives framework was first introduced to the corporate world by management guru Peter Drucker and provides a set of criteria for setting objectives. SMART provides a simple structure that acts as a checklist for creating and measuring progress towards objectives. It is such a simple and powerful tool to help create clarity around what everyone is working towards. So here's a quick reminder of what the acronym stands for:

Specific – The outcome sought needs to be expressed as specifically as possible so everyone is clear what is trying to be achieved.

Measurable – The outcome can be measured with a quantifiable metric so progress can be determined, and it's clear whether we have achieved the goal or not.

Attainable – The outcome is a stretch to make you feel challenged, but defined well enough that you can actually achieve it. It is also achievable within the constraints (resources, budgets and time) the team works with.

Relevant – Is this goal really solving the issue and aligned with your team's—and organisation's—purpose?

Time bound – The goal needs to include a time frame for when it will be achieved.

By using the SMART approach, you can create great clarity on what you are trying to achieve, by when and how success will be measured.

Out of the five criteria, I find the Attainable component to be the most challenging. Deciding whether a goal is attainable or not is like playing the dice game Tenzi and trying to balance 10 dice on top of each other – it's bloody hard. If you set your objectives too low, you could be perceived as not ambitious, chances are you won't reach your potential, results could be mediocre, and meaningful impact may not be made. On the flip side, if you set your objectives too high, then you may tune out, burn out, or like the Victorian Police Department, appear to be found out. More on this a little later.

OKRs

Objectives and Key Results (OKRs) is another approach for goal setting within teams. This approach was originally used in the 1970s by Intel, and is now used by organisations like Google, LinkedIn, Twitter and many others. The intent of the OKR approach is to identify an objective and the key results that will help achieve the objective. OKRs work best when shared publicly so that everyone is clear on what each person is working on and everyone is working to a common outcome.

Typically, teams have 3–5 high-level objectives (which roll up to department or company objectives), and under each objective there are 3–5 key measurable results. OKRs can be set in various time frames (think monthly, quarterly or annually), and progress is tracked daily as progress towards the result.

Table 5: How OKRs work from the top to the bottom

The Hierarchy of OKRs

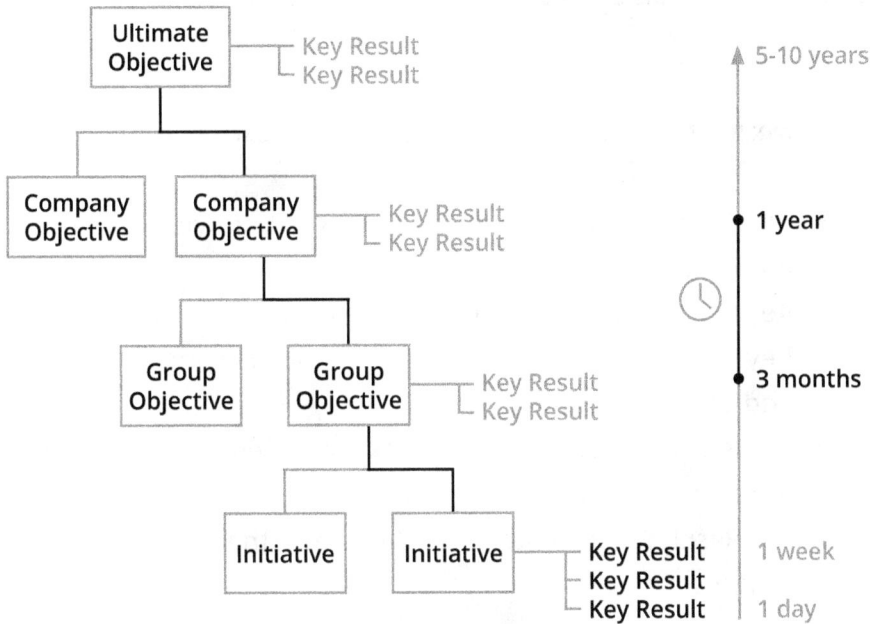

Thanks to strategy delivery platform Perdoo for
this great illustration of how OKR's work

Writing OKRs is relatively straightforward. They are similar to SMART objectives and need to tick all the boxes of a SMART goal. Your OKRs should:

- Be written on a regular cycle – for example, a quarterly basis
- Focus on the five top milestones that will make the most meaningful impact

Keep in mind the objectives represent the *intentions* and the KR (key results) are the measurable *milestones* supporting the objectives and intentions. Rob Davies, Head of Marketing for Perdoo, says, "The key results answer the question 'How do I know I'm getting there?'"

Here's an example. You want to implement new ways of working within the team and have set up a workshop to establish behaviours, rituals and routines. OKRs for this type of activity could look like this:

Objective: Improve our team dynamics over the next day, measured by:

- Key Result 1: Identifying a set of key behaviours that will enable our team to succeed
- Key Result 2: Establish team rituals for the next three months
- Key Result 3: Gain 100% commitment to trying new rituals and behaviours
- Key Result 4: Develop benchmark measurement of adherence to team behaviours
- Key Result 5: Set a date for 90 days down the track to measure progress

Imagine you are the head coach of an Olympic field hockey team. Here is what your OKRs could look like as the head coach:

Objective: Place in the top two at the Olympics

- Key Result 1: Score an average of four goals per game leading up to the final
- Key Result 2: Have more quality scoring opportunities than our opponents

- Key Result 3: Give up an average of two goals per game leading up to the final

Or for a marketing team looking to improve how customers feel about their brand:

Objective: Improve brand sentiment

- Key Result 1: Launch ATL campaign in Q2
- Key Result 2: Deliver two short-form pieces of content per week
- Key Result 3: Respond to 100% of social media comments

The key to OKRs is to be specific within a set time period and ensure all team members are aware of what each person is working on to move towards them. This will ensure the team is maximising its talent, resources and efforts.

From Table 5, OKRs work best when they start from the top and make their way down to each team. I would suggest the OKR approach can still work for your team even if the broader organisation is not using this approach. As long as the objectives are aligned to the organisation's objectives, using this framework helps create clarity for individuals and teams.

How to set objectives

There are a number of ways to set objectives and various types of objectives you can set. Let's explore how to set objectives, the impact of team objectives versus individual objectives, and the effect that objectives can have on behaviours.

So far in this chapter we have looked at some frameworks for setting objectives—SMART goals and OKRs—and we can see two primary approaches: top-down, and bottom-up.

Using the top-down method

From a top-down perspective, objectives are typically set based on historical results, predicted market conditions and the ambitions of the organisation. These objectives are then split into geographic, department or channel objectives, then allocated to a team and then to individuals. For example, a national general insurance company can set growth targets at a company level, then allocate targets at a state or channel level, then by team, and then by individual.

Pros:
- Clear and easy to communicate why targets have been set that way
- Based on historical patterns, giving people assurance of the logic behind the thinking
- Aligns priorities for everyone in the business, from the 'top to the bottom'

Cons:
- If a clear plan is not provided with the logic behind the objectives, people can become disheartened and disengaged
- If market conditions change dramatically, objectives can become unrealistic and demotivating
- High ambitions can skew reality and seem unrealistic, causing people to switch off if they feel the expectations are too high

Using the bottom-up method

Another way to set your team's objectives is to ask team members to outline what they think they can deliver. They have a good idea of what is possible and what it would take to do better. Letting team members contribute to the outcomes also creates higher levels of engagement and accountability.

A financial services state sales manager I worked with would often ask her retail store managers to forecast their annual revenue forecasts. The store managers would develop their own business plans based on the previous 12 months' foot traffic and quotes, identify new activities they could introduce to generate new quotes (for example, host a temporary sales kiosk four times a year) and think about what they could do to improve conversion rates (for example, additional coaching for new starters). They would then calculate a total sales number for the year and work towards that goal. It was impressive to see the managers' creativity and minds go to work. Because the objectives were set by the store managers, they had a higher level of belief in and commitment to achieving them.

Pros:
- Greater buy-in from the team and their staff
- A high level of transparency and understanding from and by the team
- Ambitious teams can often over-deliver on expectations from the company

Cons:
- This approach often assumes conditions will be similar to the previous year or that improvements can be made. If this is not the case, the objectives can become demotivating

- Sometimes teams will bite off more than they can chew. If unrealistic assumptions are made, motivation can be lost early
- If senior management is not authentic about receiving input, ignoring employee contributions will demotivate them and put a strain on trust levels

Regardless of which approach you take, the critical point is for each side (the higher-ups and those on the 'frontline') to have some level of give and take. The higher-ups will have access to data and trends the functional experts may not have, and the functional experts will have an understanding of current knowledge that the higher-ups might not have that could have a meaningful impact on the strategic direction and overall progress.

Individual or team objectives?

Now that we have looked at frameworks and approaches for setting objectives, we need to consider if there is an optimal balance between implementing team and individual objectives. To be honest, I'm not sure if there is an optimal balance. I know that might not be the answer you are looking for; however, I take solace in Socrates' advice: "The only true wisdom is in knowing that you know nothing." That being said, there are a number of considerations to think about when setting objectives and working through the balance between team and individual focuses.

Humans innately will look after their best interests. Although social connection is one of our fundamental needs, Maslow's Hierarchy of Needs suggests it ranks as #3, behind physiological needs (food, water, warmth and rest), and security needs (safety, shelter and stability). Researchers from Stanford University confirmed this when they looked at the impact of using different types of incentives. They found when individual incentives are used, people are less willing to be helpful to co-workers[37], and will look out for themselves over others.

So I would suggest you need to look at your team and work out: do they actually need to work together? If there is a high level of interdependence amongst the team members, then team objectives could play a larger role. If not, then team objectives may not be as important.

The benefits of placing a heavier emphasis on team objectives are that people are more likely to support each other, take the time to teach and train each other, and step up when someone is struggling. The risk of this approach is if one of the team members doesn't hold up their end and is seen as free-riding. In his study, 'Compensation and Incentives in the Workplace', Edward P Lazear found in one case that "substituting an above-average peer for a below-average peer increases a given worker's productivity by about 1 percent".[38] He also found the free-rider effect is more pronounced in small-number settings. So team size could also be a consideration. The larger the team, the less likely free-riding will impact the results.

Lazear also mentions a study undertaken by Hamilton, Nickerson and Owan (2003), who analysed a garment production plant that moved from rewarding workers at a piece rate to a team compensation rate. The authors found that average output rose by almost 20% after the switch to team production.

What about in a corporate environment? In a study with an international firm of lawyers conducted by Bartel, Cardiff-Hicks and Shaw in 2017, when team revenues were compensated instead of individual billings, senior lawyers shared much more of the work with their junior counterparts.[39] When you look at this approach, there are many benefits, including the ability for senior partners to take on more substantial work, while the junior partners have the opportunity to work on more cases, increasing their experience and knowledge.

Lazear sums up his findings: "Workers are less willing to be helpful to co-workers when the [personal] rewards are greater." So, if your objectives and compensation are tied, and individuals are remunerated only on individual outputs, the chances of people helping others is not that good.

When I look back at my time working at Novartis Pharmaceuticals, each member of the team had individual objectives that impacted our bonus results. As the table below shows, however, it served us all well to work together to grow market share across all three products.

Table 6: Team members' bonus scheme

Product	Team Member 1 bonus weighting	Team Member 2	Team Member 3
Product A	50%	35%	35%
Product B	35%	50%	15%
Product C	15%	15%	50%

Team Member 1's bonus scheme was represented by 50% of product A's results, 35% of product B's results and 15% of product C's results. Team Member 2's bonus scheme was represented by 50% of product B's results, 35% of product A's results and so on. In this case, because everyone benefited from sales across all three products, everyone worked together to drive sales across all three lines.

By taking this approach, all three team members were rewarded to ensure all three products were doing well. If Team Member 1 received feedback on product C, it made sense for them to share that information with the other team members, particularly Team Member 3 who was the team expert on that product. This would allow Team Member 3 to share learnings and Team Member 1 to get a deeper understanding of product C. It was a good example of using team objectives with modifications to the individual objectives to drive overall strong outcomes.

Stretch goals and Big Hairy Audacious Goals

Once you have determined your goal setting approach, have a think about stretch goals and BHAGs to increase performance.

Stretch goals

On top of 'regular' goals, stretch objectives are another way to motivate individuals and teams. There are a couple of views to consider when looking at the impact of stretch objectives.

Caroline Adams Miller, author of *Getting Grit*, suggests that harder objectives not only give us a greater sense of accomplishment, they also influence persistence, meaning we are more likely to achieve harder objectives than easy ones. In one of her videos, Miller talks about how she implemented a record board at a swimming club, "the largest record board ever" for this swim club. Why? Because it provided inspiration for some of the swimmers. It gave them something to strive for, something to talk about, and an opportunity to achieve something significant.

On the other hand, IBM's approach at one time was to do the opposite. According to Tim Ferriss, IBM trialled setting sales quotas markedly lower than what was expected. The result? Sales folks blew them out of the water and achieved more than what was needed. Why? As Ferriss suggests, "This approach helped sales executives feel like they were winning, which is a precursor to winning at a large scale."[40] I would guess IBM's approach in this case provided its people with the confidence to succeed, removed barriers from what could be perceived as unattainable objectives and created a high-energy workforce.

So there's a risk of setting objectives too high and a risk of setting objectives too low. Some would say small objectives encourage small thinking. Research suggests there is not one answer (sorry!). Once you agree on your objective-setting approach, then stretch objectives can come into play in whatever way suits your team. Stretch objectives can provide something higher to strive towards, to really push team members' ways of thinking and working. However, if these stretch goals are not reached, people should not be penalised, but rather rewarded for going above and beyond their current framework.

An example will help us explore these ideas. A marketing leader I worked with had a regular set of objectives to achieve within his role. He also had a stretch goal of creating an in-house creative team (a team that would make creative assets such as digital tiles and imagery for promotional materials). The in-house approach could potentially help the organisation save on external support. The organisation's approach was that if the leader didn't achieve this stretch goal, he wouldn't be penalised. However, if he was able to achieve it, even at a small scale, it would be a step in the right direction to change the way his team worked. And he would achieve a higher bonus. Over a couple of years, the in-house design team grew from one person to five and started to make an impact on savings on external supplier support expenses for not only his team but for other teams within the business as well. This is a great example of how stretch objectives with a penalty-free approach can help an organisation make meaningful progress.

Big Hairy Audacious Goals

Revenue and market share objectives may or may not excite everyone. Yes, revenue is important for survival. However, having something bigger to achieve than an annual revenue or profit target has proven to help teams achieve those targets and something more.

This is where Big Hairy Audacious Goals (BHAGs or BeeHags) come into play. Introduced by authors Jim Collins and Jerry Porras in *Building Your Company's Vision*, BHAGs are visionary and bold, and may fall into the grey area of whether or not they are achievable. They have a clear end point and if implemented correctly, will continue on regardless of who is in charge.

According to Collins and Porras, there are four types of BHAGs. You can choose:

1. A target based on a number to achieve, similar to Walmart's BHAG goal of being a US$125 billion company by the year 2000
2. A competitor BHAG, like Nike's 1960 goal to crush Adidas
3. A role model BHAG, like Giro Sport Design's 1986 BHAG of "becoming the Nike of the cycling industry"
4. An internal transformation BHAG, such as Merck's 1930 goal to transform the company from a chemical manufacturer into one of the preeminent drug-making companies in the world

Other great examples include:

- JFK's challenge to put a man on the moon: "This nation should commit itself to achieving the goal, before this decade is out, of landing a man on the moon and returning him safely to the earth"
- Microsoft's goal of putting a computer on every desk and in every home
- Volvo's goal that "no one should be killed or seriously injured in a new Volvo by 2020"
- Elon Musk's hope "someday to die on Mars, only not on impact"

When looking at these types of objectives, it's easy to understand how they help people stay focussed on the big picture. They get people excited and provide everyone with an opportunity to contribute to something bigger (and better) than a profit target. Think of the janitor at NASA who said he was helping put a man on the moon.

BHAGs don't have to be limited to organisations. Teams can also set them. When I was working in a brand team, we looked at how we could play a role in helping 250,000 children eat healthier lunches. Another health-related company wanted to help 1 million people run 5 kilometres. When considering a BHAG, keep in mind:

- BHAGs work well when they involve something the world needs or that will make it a better place. This will ensure you capture the hearts and minds of your team.
- BHAGs need to contribute to the survival of your team or company. They need to promote some sort of benefit and connection to the company.
- Ensure your BHAG is aligned with what your team is capable of achieving. By capable I don't necessarily mean what's achievable;

I mean ensuring your team has the skills, talents and resources to work towards the goal. If your team sells tyres, it might be hard to set a goal aligned with helping kids eat healthier.

• The clearer and simpler the better. Apply the 'Can a seven-year-old understand it?' rule.

The good and bad impacts of objectives on behaviours

In May 2018, the State Police in Victoria, Australia, admitted they had made a blunder. Or rather over 250,000 blunders. Over the previous five years, it was reported they faked anywhere from 250,000 to 1 million preliminary roadside alcohol breath tests.

The Victoria Police stated they didn't set quotas for breath tests, so it's intriguing as to why tests were falsified. According to the Australian Broadcasting Corporation, Professional Standards Command Assistant Commissioner Russell Barrett suspected officers faked the tests for "productivity reasons". A 'get more done quickly' approach. But if quotas weren't set, why did the fake tests happen?

Some said they happened to ensure funding for road safety was maintained. Ideally, those involved with making our roads safer could say, 'Hey, look, our work (breath testing) makes a difference! The more we test (and the more funding we get for testing), the less people drink and drive, therefore we must do a pretty good job!' If the reverse was happening, that is, the number of drink drivers was not dropping, then there could be a risk that funding could be stopped, which would mean fewer jobs or a drop in the services the Police could provide. So maybe funding and job safety drove the behaviours.

Others said it was because the objectives were not realistic or based on any logic. And some said the tests were faked because quotas did indeed need to be met. Whilst Victoria Police said it didn't set quotas for officers, some local managers did set their own targets. Police officers said faking tests was their way to deal with the demanding workloads and quotas. For example, a highway patrol unit in suburban Melbourne was meant to complete 50 breath tests in a single shift. That's on top of all their other duties, which the union said was too much. So at the end of the month, when quotas weren't being met, officers increased their focus on getting more tests done – with the trade-off being less focus on other law enforcement activities.

Now I must admit, I find the reports a little confusing. I don't understand how the head body (Victoria Police) could say there were no quotas but that lower levels of seniority would then set them. Something doesn't seem right there. But let's be real. There could have been a lot of things happening in the background we wouldn't know about. It reminds me of when Jack Nicholson's character in *A Few Good Men*, Colonel Nathan Jessep, gives testimony on whether he ordered a code red on one of his soldiers. Colonel Jessop says: "You have the luxury of not knowing what I know ... I have neither the time nor the inclination to explain myself to a man who rises and sleeps under the blanket of the very freedom that I provide and then questions the manner in which I provide it." Regardless, however, the lesson here is this: if your objectives are deemed unattainable, beware, they could end up driving the wrong behaviours.

In the case of Victoria Police, the impacts of these behaviours were serious. There would have been brand damage. Time and resources were wasted on fixing the issue. For example, as a result of the fake tests, an intelligence assessment was undertaken that involved "a very complex and protracted" analysis of 5 years of data, 1,500 preliminary breathing test devices and more than 17.7 million tests.[41] Anti-corruption units were involved. I have no doubt the stress levels for many were elevated to higher than ideal levels. Upon discovery of the practice, Victoria's Transport Accident Commission froze $4 million in road safety funding until it was satisfied the practice was no longer happening. I don't know about you, but road safety in my book is pretty important. A reduction in funding is not ideal.

Sharing objectives

We've talked a lot about setting objectives, which is really important. It's also important to share them with your team and others.

I could never understand why some teammates wouldn't share their objectives, scorecards or however they measured their impacts with each other. More often than not, if people understand what everyone's working towards, they find opportunities to support each other and collectively achieve their objectives, and maybe even more!

When I was leading a sponsorship team in a marketing department, one of my colleagues was responsible for driving traffic to a new website. He had set up a new online information hub with the intent of providing useful information to our customers. His objective was to get people to visit the site at least once. To do this, he had to create awareness of the hub. If people were aware of the hub, and the information was useful, people would see our company in good light, and down the track consider us for our products.

As a sponsorship team, our goal was to improve key brand metrics to help solidify our company's position. The sponsorship team would partner up with mass participation events (think of large fun runs) and professional sporting teams to help support the needs of the participants and fans and make them aware of how we could help them. For some reason, it took our two teams nearly 18 months to get to a point where we realised we could actually help each other. The new hub could take advantage of our sponsorship assets to help create interesting and useful content, and the sponsorship team could use the hub as another proof-point of how we could help existing and potential customers. Once we started to share our objectives with each other, we were able to get much more bang for our buck with our sponsorship assets and contribute a large number of visitors to the new website. Thinking back, it seems absurd that it took us so long to work better together and realise our objectives were similar.

Sharing objectives and helping your national sports team perform better

So what happens when you are clear on your objectives and you share them with others, even with an external party? It can mean giving your favourite national team a better chance of winning.

One of Bupa's objectives was to demonstrate how they were making a difference to the health and care of Australians. Back in 2016, one of their sponsorship partners was Cricket Australia. At this stage the Bupa brand had been in the Australian market for just under six years and was still a relatively young brand in the $20 billion health insurance industry.

For the non-cricket fans out there, Cricket Australia (CA) is the governing body for cricket in Australia, from grassroots development to elite player pathways, national teams and national professional leagues. Cricket Australia also runs professional leagues such as the Women's and Men's T20 Big Bash League. In Canada, it's similar to a combination of Hockey Canada and the National Hockey League. Or in America, like Baseball America and Major League Baseball.

Similar to most professional codes, Cricket Australia has a high performance team that is responsible for creating elite pathways for athletes from juniors to seniors, all working towards producing the best male and female Australian cricket teams. The high performance team is also accountable for the country's global performance rankings. One of the support teams within the high performance team is the Sports Science and Medical (SS&M) team. The SS&M team is made up of some of the best doctors, physiotherapists and sports scientists in the country, and maybe even the world. This group of folks is pretty clear on their objective – to ensure as many players as possible are healthy enough to play for the national team when needed.

Back to 2016. As the sophistication of sports science improved, the SS&M team started to collect large amounts of data on the players. To do so was initially a tricky process. Cricket Australia was following 270 national and state players on a regular basis. Throughout the year, players competed in various national, international and professional competitions. In addition to collecting national players' data, the SS&M team needed to convince local state associations to ensure their players were tracking their data as well in case they were called up to participate in the national program. Eventually Cricket Australia developed a bespoke app to collect the data, allowing players around the world to share their information with the SS&M team.

The team collected data such as number of balls bowled (thrown), types of balls bowled, performance against opponents, location, time of day, age, height, weight of players, velocity and spin rates of balls thrown, number of consecutive days played, recovery periods, travel time … and the list goes on. They also tracked wellbeing data. Things like sleep quantity and quality and how well the players felt. Whilst they had a large pool of data, it wasn't necessarily solving all their headaches. After eight years of collecting data, as they stated, "we had so much data we often question what to do with it all".

From Bupa's perspective, the partnership with Cricket Australia represented an opportunity to maximise national brand awareness (cricket is arguably Australia's most popular professional sport, played across the entire country). To gain national awareness, Bupa had signage at televised games to gain exposure through broadcasts, and logos on the coaching and medical team to associate themselves with strong team support. They also organised player appearances to support various marketing campaigns.

Through a desire to demonstrate their health expertise, Bupa explored opportunities to support the men's and women's Australian cricket teams' health needs. Bupa knew a lot about health, and CA cricketers needed to be healthy. It seemed beneficial to find some common ground. By sharing Bupa's objective of demonstrating their health expertise with the broader Cricket Australia organisation and vice versa, Bupa was able to help the SS&M team use the data they were collecting in a much more meaningful way.

Bupa had a health analytics department, headed up by David Cross. The teams were able to work together and make good inroads into supporting the players' health. As David said, "One of the things we were able to determine is when players rank how they feel with a scoring system of zero to five. If for three days in a row players score themselves a three or less, we've been able to link that to a higher risk of injury. And vice versa: if you score three or higher for three days in a row your risk of injury drops significantly."

That's pretty powerful information. If a player scored themselves a three or less for three consecutive days, an automatic email would be sent to the coaching staff and the SS&M team, triggering the opportunity for them to have a conversation with the player and potentially alter their training program.

As Alex Kountouris, CA's Science and Sports Medicine Manager, said: "By changing the activities for say a week or two, and then getting them back into action, we can be confident of avoiding injuries that may have been previously caused a player to be out of action for up to six weeks or more."[42]

Imagine the impact on the player, the team and all the fans if star players are able to play more games at a healthier level. Cricket Australia (and their fans) are happier because they can work better to field the best team, and Bupa is happy because they are able to demonstrate their expertise with a strong and engaging proof-point.

And all because of a simple act of sharing and creating clarity on their objectives.

Once you have your team and individual objectives, share them with others. Share them with your colleagues, other teams and other departments. By being clear up front on what you are trying to achieve, you increase the chances of others being able to support you so you can make meaningful progress.

Key Takeaways

☑ When setting objectives, ensure there is logic behind them. If not, they may be unattainable and drive the wrong behaviours. As much as I like the pop rock band Imagine Dragons' song 'Whatever It Takes', I don't believe doing whatever it takes to achieve a goal is applicable if it means compromising ethical behaviour.

☑ To ensure you get the best return on efforts and investments, ensure your teams share their objectives with each other – at a team level and an individual level. This will help identify opportunities to support each other, leverage strengths and minimise duplication of efforts.

☑ There are a number of different approaches to setting objectives. Big Hairy Audacious Goals are often the most effective way to win the hearts and minds of your team and can result in making a positive difference in the world.

Reflections

💡 How many of your team members are across each other's objectives for the year? Who has seen whose 'scorecards'? What other departments or organisations might benefit from knowing your objectives?

💡 How could you make your objectives—or your team's objectives—more inspiring? What's one Big Hairy

Audacious Goal you could set as a team for the next six months?

* What less-than-ideal behaviours MIGHT your team's objectives be driving?

CHAPTER 12

Creating clarity with roles and responsibilities

The American sitcom *The Office* is a pretty funny show depicting the everyday life of working in an office. There is a great episode in the fifth season where Dwight becomes frustrated with the lack of engagement from his colleagues in his fire safety seminar. He stages a fake fire in the office to demonstrate the importance of knowing who does what in the event of a real one. Chaos erupts, resulting in one of the employees attempting to escape by crawling through an air duct and crashing down through the ceiling not far from where they started. Ouch.

The scene demonstrates what people do—and don't do—when they aren't clear on who is responsible for what, particularly when stress levels are high.

Being clear on roles and responsibilities can help avoid chaos. Data scientist Lieke Pijnacker from Effectory undertook some research into roles and responsibilities. In his study, he found that nearly 50% of employees across various sectors lacked role clarity. He also reported "employees who experience role clarity are 53% more efficient and that overall work performance increases by 25%".[43] Impressive. By understanding who is responsible for what, teams can remain focussed on what is important and coordinate everyone's efforts, abilities and strengths to achieve individual, team and company goals.

In an article published in 2012 in the *Harvard Business Review*, author Tammy Erikson suggested that without clear role descriptions employees are more likely to waste their energies negotiating their roles within their teams rather than focussing on their productive tasks. This often leads to unnecessary politics-playing, turf wars and a lack of productivity.

Table 7: The impact of unclear and clear roles and responsibilities

Unclear	IMPACTS ON	Clear
Minimal	Progress	Meaningful
Depleted	Energy	Renewed
Turf wars	Focus	Goals
Declines	Engagement	Rises
The wrong picture	Connection	To the big picture
Scattered	Personal development	Focussed
Up and down	Morale	Steady

Why is it so hard?

In an increasingly dynamic and connected global economy, new businesses are constantly being created and existing businesses are re-inventing themselves. In response, jobs and job roles have been changing at a frenetic pace. Employers are expected to meet and embrace these changes, but often without any consideration of what the new role expectations are for employees.

~ Adapt by Design[44]

The idea of creating clear roles and responsibilities sounds practical and simple. Being clear on roles and responsibilities is like using the express lane in a supermarket – it saves you time and gets you where you want to be much more quickly.

Bill Parcells, legendary National Football League coach, got it right. There are several stories about how Parcells explained each player's role to them. In one story, he would go to a defensive lineman and say to him, "Your job this Sunday is to put number 96 on his ass. Forget about the ball, forget about the quarterback. You will be successful if on every play I look over and I see #96 on his ass." Seems pretty simple, doesn't it.

However, it's not that easy. And there aren't that many jobs where it's as straightforward as putting #96 on his ass. Why not? There is a range of factors that contribute to a lack of clarity on roles and responsibilities, including the size of an organisation, the location of teams, assumptions, trust (or lack of), resourcing and overlapping objectives. Despite these challenges, it its possible— and important—to create as much clarity as you can with your team's roles and responsibilities.

Position descriptions are only the beginning

Ben Oliver is a high performance executive in Australia and former High Performance Manager for the Western Australia Cricket Association (WACA). He described to me how his team started out with some structure around roles and responsibilities with position descriptions (PDs). Over time, as they understood each other's strengths, they revisited the roles and responsibilities and adjusted their original plan. "The roles and responsibilities changed over time because we identified certain people had certain strengths that, as a team, we could leverage," shared Ben. "It didn't matter if it was part of the original scope of the PD – we were able to be dynamic and evolve over time."

What I love about Ben's story is that the team agreed on a starting point (the structure around who was responsible for what with a PD). They then got stuck into the work and, over time, identified ways they could do things better. Because they had an open mindset to doing things differently, they were able to leverage strengths as they got to know each other. Result? While Ben was at the WACA, the team won three national Big Bash League men's titles, were runners up twice with the women's squad, had two men's domestic one-day tournament wins, and were runners up in two Shield finals and a Women's National Cricket League play-off.

Position descriptions are like buying a used car. You are told something about the car (or job). The intention is right. You do your research and build up your confidence that it's right for you. Others give you their thoughts of what you can expect. But until you're in the driver's seat for a while, you don't really know what you are getting into.

Position descriptions can provide some initial clarity on the boundaries of a person's responsibilities and expectations, and provide a reference point for how an employee spends her time at work on a daily basis, with who and what success looks like.

The challenge with job descriptions is that certain tasks within the descriptions—or the whole description itself—can become quickly redundant. As HR and management consultant Susan Heathfield says, "Job descriptions can become outdated in a fast-paced, changing, customer-driven work environment."[45] Whilst the purpose of the document is to create clarity for individuals, teams and stakeholders, keep in mind they are created *in* a moment of time based on what's known *at* that time. At best, they are based on the current customer needs, the current business needs and the current business structure.

Like Ben and his colleagues at the WACA, it's important to initially agree on who will do what. It's just as important for teams to have a process in place to create ongoing clarity for roles and responsibilities.

An ongoing process for creating clarity

The AAA process—Align, Assess, Adjust—can help create clarity within your team initially, and then on an ongoing basis. Following these three steps over a period of time will help you create clarity on who does what.

Table 8: AAA process of creating clarity of roles and responsibilities

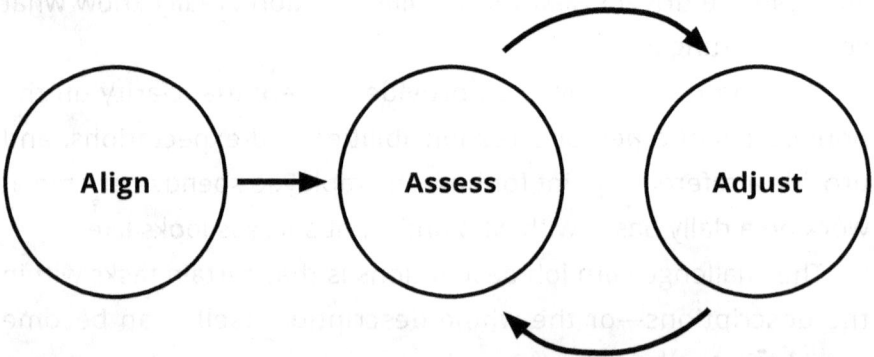

Step 1 Establish Alignment: Create a starting point for what each team member should be doing and make sure everyone is as clear as

possible. Acknowledge that this starting point may not be perfect and commit to working through the imperfections throughout the year.

Step 2 Assess: Choose a period of time—I recommend doing this at least twice a year—and check in a few times to see what's changed, what hasn't changed, and what needs to change.

Step 3 Adjust: Following the assessment, agree on what could change to put your team in a better position to achieve more.

This process can be undertaken at a team, individual and project level.

How to create initial alignment amongst teams

The audience for any position description is often the person taking the role and their manager, and that's it. It could also include team members and peers. In some organisations I've worked in, draft PDs are shared with key stakeholders as a good engagement activity; gaining inputs helps ensure the broader group is on the same page and allows any amendments to be made to avoid future clashes. To create some initial alignment, take these two steps:

1. As the leader, share the PD with your team prior to a new person starting in a role.
2. Ensure that when someone new starts in the team, everyone has a chance to meet them one-to-one to understand what they believe their role and responsibilities to be, and how that impacts each existing team member.

How to create clarity across interdepartmental teams and projects

There are two great tools—RACIs and RATSIs—for gaining clarity on roles and responsibilities for more complex work when it is vital for the group to understand who is responsible for each component of the deliverables and how the team will work together. For example, there may be tasks to be completed by various individuals, across different teams and departments. You may also have a variety of stakeholders who need to be across what's happening. RACIs and RATSIs help everyone understand who is responsible for what. These tools can also be used more than once with the lifespan of a team, for example at the beginning of a project to create alignment or later to assess if an adjustment is required.

RACI matrix

RACI is an acronym for Responsible, Accountable, Consulted and Informed. Each letter of RACI represents who is responsible for what, and is often represented in a table format.

Table 9: RACI matrix

Tasks	Responsible	Accountable	Consulted	Informed
Task 1				
Task 2				
Task 3				

Responsible

Those who are identified as *Responsible* are the folks who do the work and complete a task or objective. It's important to note that more than one person can be *Responsible*. Ensure there are enough cooks in the kitchen to do the work, but not too many.

Accountable

The individual who is *Accountable* is ultimately the person who ensures the task is delivered to a certain level of satisfaction or standard. In the majority of cases, only one person can be Accountable as they provide the final sign-off, approval or nod that a task is deemed complete. They have veto power and are ultimately accountable for the successful delivery or implementation. This individual must also make sure all responsibilities are assigned in the matrix for all related activities. Again, stick to one person being accountable. If not, decisions will be delayed and progress will stall. And there will probably be a lot more swearing about each other.

Consulted

Those who are *Consulted* are required to provide input before any of the tasks are finalised. These people are usually subject matter experts or people who will be impacted by the tasks, decisions or outcomes of the work; their input is required to ensure the tasks are done appropriately. There is a fine balance between who needs to be consulted and who needs to be informed. Be somewhat ruthless with who falls in the *Consulted* box over the *Informed* box, otherwise you may find you need to satisfy too many people, which will again delay progress and make things more complicated than they need to be.

Informed

Those who are *Informed* are those who need to be kept in the loop as an FYI. They could be key stakeholders who need to be across what's happening, but don't directly contribute to the task at hand. For example, a customer service call centre team could be informed of a new TV ad going live, however they would not be involved in any decision-making about the creative, messaging or delivery of the project.

Here is an example of a completed RACI. To ensure everyone is clear on the outcomes of this exercise, it is best completed with all relevant stakeholders in the room.

Table 10: A completed RACI matrix for the delivery of a marketing campaign

Job to be done: Deliver a marketing campaign

Tasks	Responsible	Accountable	Consulted	Informed
Brief an agency	Marketing Manager	Head of Marketing	Head of Sales	Director of Sales
Agree on concept	Marketing Manager	Director of Marketing	Head of Marketing, Director of Sales, legal team	Director of Customer Service
Create the TV ad	Marketing Agency	Head of Marketing	Director of Marketing, Marketing Manager	n/a
Inform key stakeholders of timing and media plans	Marketing Manager, Head of Marketing	Director of Marketing	Director of Sales	Director of Customer Service

RATSI

Another type of visual roles and responsibility matrix is a RATSI, which stands for Responsible, Authority, Task, Support and Informed. This model typically uses the first three letters—the 'RAT'—most of the time. Some people like this model because it clearly defines who has final decision-making authority, and the difference between the *Responsible* and *Accountable* fields is clearer than in the RACI.

Responsible
Those who are *Responsible* ensure the work is done and done appropriately. They may not necessarily do the work, but at minimum oversee that the work is done properly.

Authority
The person marked as Authority has the final decision-making authority on the work. They are not involved in the day-to-day work.

Task
The *Task* refers to the individual/group that will actually do the work. The *Responsible* individual typically oversees the *Task* and will support where required.

Support
This refers to those who support the *Task* person to get the work done. Ideally the *Task* is the lone person who does the actual task, but at times support is required. When this is the case, a *Support* is identified.

Informed

This group or individual is informed the work is going to happen, is happening and has finished.

Using these two frameworks—RACI and RATSI—could help you create initial alignment and clarity. The key word here is initial. Be ready for things to change and to assess how they will need to work moving forward.

Assessing clarity of roles and responsibilities team exercise

One key to creating higher performing teams is to ensure your team reviews roles and responsibilities regularly. At least once a year, depending on how fast your industry or company changes. My Circle of Clarity exercise will help with the review process.

The Circle of Clarity team exercise helps team members gain an understanding of each other's roles. It's a great exercise to do on an annual or semi-annual basis as priorities change throughout the year. Here's how to do it.

1. The team sits in a circle, with one person in the middle.
2. Everyone around the circle writes down on an index card what they believe the person in the middle is responsible for, as does the person in the middle. Encourage the team to be as descriptive as possible, including key stakeholders, what components of tasks the person is responsible for and measurements of success.
3. Each person around the circle then shares what they believe the middle person's role and responsibilities include. The person in the middle then shares what they believe their role and responsibilities are and the differences are discussed.

4. Allocate 5–10 minutes for each individual in the middle.
5. To help visual learners, you can use Post-it notes instead of index cards and put everyone's responses on the wall, or ask a scribe to record the responses to provide a visual.
6. It's important to focus the discussion on the role instead of the person. This will help avoid any personal attacks or biases, while allowing the discussion to help uncover some misalignments. If further discussion is needed beyond the allocated time, make a point for those involved in that discussion to pick up within the next 48 hours.

Assessing role clarity when a new person joins the team

Any time a new role is introduced there can be a misalignment of understanding who is responsible for what. This often causes confusion, frustration, wasted time and a lack of meaningful progress. Not to mention the drain on mental energy that comes with such confusion. This lack of clarity impacts both team members and their stakeholders.

Getting things right seems to be a challenge for me, but I am happy to say I did get something right. In one of my roles, a new position was created that would work very closely with me (we were peers, reporting into the same manager). When my new colleague arrived, I locked us in a room early on for a good session so we could agree on who would be responsible for what. We were able to identify the black and the white of who did what—'You do this, I do that'—and the grey. The grey being ... 'Hmmm, not sure who could do this, let's start here and as things come up, we can talk about them and adjust as need be.' As it turned out, this was one of the best working relationships I have had. Our teams delivered some great outcomes and pushed the boundaries on how things were done.

When there is crossover about who does what between two individuals, there are often some components of black and white. However, where it gets confusing is what I call the grey bits – and the grey is where the headaches begin and sometimes linger. So what can you do to avoid the grey bits? Nothing really. But you can manage them, with my BGW (Black – Grey – White) Framework.

All you need is a room, some paper or a whiteboard to draw out three columns, some writing utensils, a willingness to discuss and an open mind.

Step 1: Draw three columns with the headers 'The Black' (referring to one person's or team's job), 'The Grey', and 'The White' (referring to a second person's or team's job). It can look a little something like this:

Table 11: The BGW Framework for creating clarity on roles and responsibilities

The Black (Job A or Team A)	The Grey (the uncertain)	The White (Job B or Team B)

Step 2: Agree on what is clearly one person's (or team's) responsibilities in the Black column. And do the same with the other person's responsibilities in the White column.

Step 3: When you come up with an activity you are not sure about or cannot agree on initially, put it in the Grey column. Avoid trying to work out who is responsible for the grey area initially. But when there is any uncertainty, look to clarify exactly what each of you is talking about. 'When you say you are responsible for X, what exactly do you mean when say X?' And when you get X, write it down in the middle. The clearer the two of you can get on what those responsibilities mean, the greater understanding you'll create and the more you'll be able to agree on those responsibilities.

The more specific you can get the better. A well-known Australian Football Rules coach is renowned for making his players' roles and responsibilities as clear as possible. Typically teams are split into positions. One of those positions is a midfielder who is responsible for the ball as it moves through the middle of the field. To create clarity for his midfielders, the coach has designated some midfielders as blue midfielders, some orange and some white. Blue midfielders are instructed to err on the side of being offensively minded, meaning if they think the ball is going to move into the opponent's zone, they can start to position themselves in the event the ball does come forward. The white midfielders are the opposite – they will err on the side of being too defensive. The orange midfielders have to do both: they need to go hard when the ball is moving forward, but also need to bust their chops to get back when the ball is coming back.

This level of detail has many implications. Firstly, the players are clear on how to play and what instincts to use or tamper down. If I am a white midfielder, I know I have to play conservatively. Secondly, this type of approach helps for succession planning and drafting. If I know I need an orange midfielder, I need to look for players who can run a longer distance at a higher pace than say a blue midfielder.

Back to our four steps to create clarity using the BGW Framework. The outcome of the first three steps is that you'll gain an appreciation of what you each do and you'll create momentum by, at minimum, gaining some understanding and ideally some agreement. Once you've filled in the three columns, the next step is to work out the Grey section.

Step 4: Work out and agree how those Grey responsibilities will be split. Make proposals, suggest ideas, look to give more than take. Be totally honest about why you believe what you do. If you want a certain task to be with you because it's a development area for you, say so. If you want more power, people and resources, share it ... but be prepared to shift your thinking as your ego isn't necessarily the best reason to make a decision. Talk about the implications of these decisions with your team member. You'll find that you'll be able to start shifting some of the items in the Grey column to either the Black or the White. And you know what this is? Progress. Meaningful progress. Well done.

Now, if you are like Merlin the Magician and you can completely eliminate the Grey column, high five. Chances are you'll still have some areas that are unresolved or you may not know the best way to move forward. That's ok. The key now is to make a commitment to each other that when something comes up in this space you'll pick up the phone or walk over to each other and run it by the other person and ask what they think the best way to move forward is. More times than not, you'll find that:

1. Both parties will find a way to resolve the issue or opportunity together, and you'll hear phrases like, 'That's a great idea', 'Keep going with it' and 'Keep me in the loop' or
2. One person may not have the capacity to take on the task. You may hear things like, 'That could work – keep going, we have other priorities but don't let that hold us back' or
3. You may be able to support each other: 'I like that idea', 'Why don't I get Alex to work with you on this because she did something similar before and could do X, Y and Z for you'

Will this approach solve every issue? Maybe. Maybe not. At minimum it creates greater clarity around what and why things are being done the way they are. Whether you agree or not is another story. Chances are when you create clarity, you'll be able to make better progress and start to spend less time worrying (and swearing) about what's happening – because at minimum you'll know. And if you can work together to agree on a couple of extra items, you'll be in a better position than where you were to begin with.

Adjusting for a new level of clarity

Great work, you've completed the assessment stage of creating greater clarity around your and your team's roles and responsibilities. You've spoken – now what action do you need to take? This is where you can make adjustments.

Robert Half, the late founder of employment agency Robert Half International, once said, "The ego trip is a journey to nowhere." When discussing changes or adjustments to roles and responsibilities, do so with a growth mindset. It's not always easy to just 'choose' a growth mindset, however if you can look at any adjustments as an opportunity to grow while supporting the growth of someone else, chances are meaningful progress can be made. Yes, some people will be on a power trip and want to do it all because they know best. Or because they want the glory, power or resources. Making adjustments doesn't mean you have to give them all the power or do it their way, but if you show a willingness to change, they may reciprocate. You need to decide what's important to you and where you want to stand your ground. The great thing is that this is what you can control when making adjustments: identifying what's important to you, how you present what's important to you, and how you respond depending on whether you get what you want or not.

The most effective tool for all three stages

If you want to save time and angst, and put yourself and your team in the best position to understand your roles and what you need to deliver, use the best tool of all time: dialogue. Talk. Ask questions. Explore. Clarify. And be curious and open. Whilst RACI and RATSI matrices help provide visual representations of clarity, the best tool any team can use is dialogue. As Sandy Pentland from MIT confirmed in 'The New Science of Building Great Teams', speaking face-to-face is the most effective way for teams to communicate. The same goes with creating clarity when it comes to roles and responsibilities. Whether it's with your team, your colleagues, your peers in other departments or your boss, making time to align and establish as clear as possible who is responsible for what could be the most effective piece of work you do for your team.

Key Takeaways

☑ As the economy shifts quickly, businesses need to continue to reinvent themselves. This means what people do and how they do it may need to change to. To ensure everyone is on the same page about who is doing what, get together with your team at least once a year to review roles and responsibilities.

☑ There are a number of tools to help create clarity on roles and responsibilities, including the BGW, RACI, RATSI and Circle of Clarity frameworks.

☑ The best tool of all is dialogue. Discuss the areas of contention—or the grey areas—and be open to changing your perspective on how things can be done.

Reflections

🔆 Think about a time when there was a lack of clarity around roles and responsibilities. What did it cost you and your team? Think about how much time was wasted (and translate that into dollars). How much mental energy was wasted and what outcomes did you miss out on?

🔆 When you think about roles and responsibilities in your team, where could you create a higher level of clarity that would save you and your team time, pain and energy?

🔆 When was the last time you sat down with your team to assess and potentially realign roles and responsibilities?

CHAPTER 13

Creating clarity with behaviours

Every year I see my doctor to get my blood checked. During one of my visits, everything looked good, except my cholesterol levels. My doctor started to explain what cholesterol was and the difference between high-density lipoprotein and low-density lipoprotein. I didn't really get it (what am I, a doctor?). So she broke it down in layman's terms for me:

> Imagine your artery as a tube where blood flows through. Within the artery, there is cholesterol that is produced naturally and from your diet. Picture the good cholesterol—HDL—they are bigger balls of cholesterol. Bad cholesterol are smaller balls of cholesterol.
>
> The big balls, they get moved along your arteries and protect your arteries from shrinking. But the small ones, when you get too many small balls in your artery, the balls start to make their way into the lining of the artery. At first, these little balls don't make too much of an impact. Over time though, those balls start to add up, and eventually can block the artery. Which is bad.

Bad indeed. Now I can honestly say, like Al Pacino in *Any Given Sunday*, it's the difference between living and dying.

When I thought about it, I realised behaviours are like cholesterol. Bad ones will always be there. It's human nature. However, if they accumulate over time, bad behaviours become blockers. They can make good behaviours redundant and cause a lot of damage.

The C word

I have resisted using the C word so far. However, I will give in. Culture. Culture is made of many components. The more I delve into what culture is, talk to people about it and try to come up with a definition of it, the more confused I get. There are so many approaches to what culture is. One thing I will say though – a company's 'culture' is often driven by the behaviour of its people. And whilst it usually starts at the top, behaviours within teams themselves can be the difference between a team that is shining and a team that is self-serving.

In 2017, the National Bureau of Economic Research in the US released a study involving 1,348 North American firms. The survey found that more than half of their senior executives see corporate culture as one of the top three drivers of their company's value, with 92% of respondents saying company value would increase by improving culture. And a mere 16% said their culture 'is where it should be'.

These stats baffle me. To me, this is an example of talking the talk, but not walking the talk. If the culture isn't where it could be, what's being done to get it where it should be?

Here's one suggestion.

Start with identifying the behaviours you and your team believe are the keys to success. Keep it simple. Talk about them. Bring them to life. Live by them. Make them non-negotiable.

What are your team's big rocks?

From my doctor's cholesterol balls, let's talk about Glenn Stewart's rocks. Glenn heads up the high performance team of the West Coast Eagles Australian Football Club, and he talks about big rocks:

> Often you hear of teams looking for the one percenters. Our approach at the club is to ensure we focus on the big rocks first, then concern ourselves about one percenters once we are satisfied the big rocks are in place. By big rocks, I mean what are the two, three maybe four things we need to do really well to win. If we can get those things right, we believe it will be very difficult for anyone to take us down.

> In the AFL, teams started to invest heavily into taking their teams over to the USA for high altitude training. It's a costly investment in terms of dollars and time. We looked at our group and asked ourselves – is high altitude training a big rock? Or is investing in additional support for our playing group, say for example, a kicking coach, a better option? We know kicking skills are critical to winning and thus a big rock. So we decided to invest in kicking instead of following the trend and going to the States.

You remember Heidi Clarris, the experience leader from Bupa we met earlier whose team was sinking for a time? One of the critical behaviours she witnessed in her team was the lack of disagreement expressed between team members. They all felt comfortable telling her about their disagreements. But they were reluctant to share their concerns with each other. The team eventually realised what Heidi knew all along – this lack of communication was delaying any sort of meaningful progress. It was also causing unnecessary frustration.

I spent another afternoon with Heidi's team and we reviewed the results from the AB Team Dynamics Assessment they had completed. The AB Team Dynamics Assessment is an online tool I created, based on research, team models and nearly 20 years of working in teams. It's 360-degree feedback for the team, from the team. The results identify what the team agrees is going well, what they agree is not going well ... and more importantly what's not being said. I have yet to come across a team that does not have any issues brewing. The difference between shining teams and the other types of teams is that teams that talk about their issues knock them on the head before they become real issues. My assessment tool is a bridge for teams. A bridge from 'I'm not 100% comfortable sharing what I really think' to 'I'm happy to share my thoughts in the assessment and discuss why I think our results are low with the team.'

After completing the assessment, Heidi's team recognised there were issues brewing about whether they were sharing what they really thought and how they can provide each other with feedback. Through a facilitated discussion, team members opened up, dropped their guard and started to have 'real-er conversations'. The outcome was that the team came up with a number of new behaviours they promised to commit to.

Table 12: Promises developed by Heidi's team in their workshop

We promise to Use the Levers. This means we will:
- Accept that at times we will need a captain's call to make decisions quickly
- Genuinely back whatever team decision is made
- Ask 'why' more often

We promise to Say it Sooner. This means we will:
- Have difficult, open and honest conversations early – as soon as issues/concerns arise
- Avoid nodding to be nice

We promise to Nurture and Grow. This means we will:
- Draw on strengths, grow and recognise each other through open, honest feedback
- Listen as much as we talk
- Be vulnerable and supportive of others when they are vulnerable with us

We promise to Respect the Human. This means we will:
- Respect the human over the deadline – and trust the result will be better
- Prioritise our own and each other's Performance Energy

We promise to remember 'Rule #6!' This means we will:
- Not take ourselves too seriously

The impact was immediate, and by that I mean changes were made the next day. The promise to say it sooner made the biggest impact straight away. In meetings, teammates were saying 'I need to say something sooner' and 'Can I say something sooner?' Another bridge to safety had been built. These words turned into action. The team was saying things sooner. They were agreeing to use the levers to make quicker decisions. Three months later, when we assessed how far the team had come, the results were as follows.

Table 13: Results of the progress Heidi's team made with their promised team behaviours

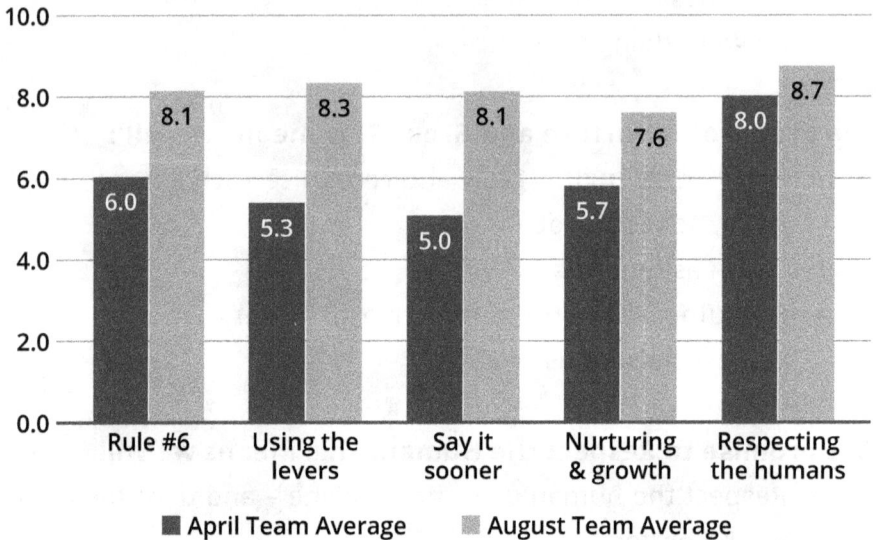

A 62% improvement in saying it sooner, 57% increase in using the levers, and over 30% improvement on Rule #6 and Nurturing and Growth. Boom! From a delivery point of view, the team also re-established where they could make the biggest impact and through a number of tough but productive discussions, were able to get more clarity about what the focus of their work needed to be.

Later in the year, Heidi and the team took the opportunity to reflect on how far they had come and acknowledged the transformation of their team approach. Heidi said: "I used to dread team meetings (as did others) and now we embrace them and have a lot of fun. It is very clear that everyone is comfortable not only to be the person they are but also to enjoy the differences that others bring. We are actually all really good friends."

"Since we started together, we not only carved out a niche for ourselves in a cluttered Customer Experience landscape we also delivered more than we set out to achieve."

Friends, over-delivering and fun. Sounds good to me, Heidi.

Heidi's team's decision to align to an agreed set of specified behaviours is one example of what can happen when a team focusses on critical behaviours for success. Another example comes from the accounting software world.

MYOB is a major player in the accounting software industry, and their service and support team has played a large role in the company's success. In 2019 I was engaged to work with one of their leadership teams. Together we identified three new behaviours to improve how they could reach the potential of their group: Speak Out, Reach Out and Break Out. By Speaking Out (sharing more feedback sooner), Reaching Out (checking in with all members of the team on a formal and informal basis) and Breaking Out (ensuring team members had some less formal time together, such as kicking off meetings with non-work items), they became much more comfortable in sharing personal challenges. That's putting it mildly – their likelihood to share personal challenges went up by 150% over 3 months. Their confidence in giving feedback to each other also lifted by 60% and their ability to ask each other for help improved by 39%. Boom! Tim Williams, the team's leader, also noticed a change in the discussions he was having with his team: "The team is talking together much more than before. And for me, I hear far less about any issues my team are having amongst each other. Which I love, because I can focus on bigger picture items. And this all came because we were able to collectively agree on what's important and put it into action." Focus on the big rocks.

How jumping in a Bentley does not help install the right behaviours

In his book *Gridiron Genius*, Michael Lombardi shares the story of Jim Mora, the head coach of the Atlanta Falcons in America's National Football League. During training camp, one of the team's best players, DeAngelo Hall, had a new purchase delivered to him – a new Bentley. As you do. The new rig happened to arrive on the day the team was heading out to a team bowling night. Mora had asked all players to take the team bus as it was a team bonding session. However, once the Bentley arrived, as Lombardi recounts, Hall was keen to choose his new wheels over taking the bus (I can kind of understand where he was coming from, can't you?).[46]

"Instead of sending a message that no one is above the team, not even when it comes to an off-season social event, [Coach] Mora chose to appease his star," explained Lombardi. "Making matters worse, Mora chose to drive shotgun." In the Bentley. Not the team bus.

What message did this behaviour send? Apparently not the right one. "Playing favourites poisoned the dressing room," suggested Lombardi, "and bending the rule eroded Mora's authority." The outcome: Mora was fired six months later, cutting his multimillion-dollar contract short by two years.

Compare Coach Mora's behaviours to the ones of Richard Bowden, former CEO of Bupa Australia and New Zealand. Richard did not believe it was in the best interest of his customers to be spending the company's (or as he put it, his customers') money on lavish dinners or even something as simple as a cup of coffee during staff meetings. Particularly when the company was going through difficult times. The story goes like this: During his first meeting with his marketing executive, Bowden's EA popped in and asked if anyone wanted a coffee. 'Hell yeah' responded the marketing executive (well that's not what she said, but I thought it sounded better than 'Yes please'!). Bowden then pulled $10 from his wallet and handed it to his EA. The act of pulling his money from his wallet—instead of his corporate credit card—sent a message right away to his marketing executive. When he said 'we' need to tighten up on our discretionary spending, he meant it for everyone, including himself. He didn't expense the coffee – he paid for it from his own pocket. His marketing executive relayed this experience to her team, which resulted in her team reviewing their use of corporate credit cards, and so the impact spread across the whole marketing team.

Being a leader is not easy, we all agree. To do it well, you need to lead by example. Whichever behaviours your team chooses – you need to ensure that as the leader, you are living, breathing and upholding them as agreed.

As Lombardi commented at the conclusion of his story about Mora, "When rules don't apply to everyone, the ensuing chaos collapses whatever foundation a leader has tried so hard to build."

Making behaviours stick

In golf there's a saying about driving for show, putting for dough. The idea is that anyone who can hit a monster drive is a great showman, however when it comes to making a good score, it all comes down to how well you can putt. If you can putt, you can win. When making your agreed behaviours stick, the same applies.

How often do you sit in team meetings or a 'top 100 leaders' get-together and people talk the talk but you know damn right it's all for show? When it comes to 'doing' the behaviours, for some, it just doesn't happen. The good thing is that for the most part, those who do more talking than doing are usually found out. Not always but often. And for those who aren't found out, I like to believe they stub their toe or inadvertently bite their tongue more often than others.

If there's a takeaway for making behaviours work across a team, it's this. You can talk for show. Or do for dough.

So let's get stuck into the dough. Check out the costs of bad dough – poor behaviours:

- Employees who experience poor management are more likely to have a heart attack in the next decade.[47]
- Roughly 80% of women who've been harassed leave their jobs within two years.[48]
- Research shared by SafeWork Australia shows that depression, psychological distress and emotional exhaustion are common outcomes for bullied workers.[49]
- Removing a toxic worker from your organisation can deliver twice the benefit of adding a 'superstar'.[50]

Using the GAP Team Behavioural Model to make behaviours stick

Once your team is aligned on the behaviours which will drive success, it's time to close the gap between what's happening now and what needs to happen. That's where my GAP Team Behavioural Model comes in. GAP stands for:

- Group focus
- Accountability (individual)
- Patience

The Gap Team Behavioural Model can help ensure the behaviours identified become behaviours actioned so meaningful progress is made.

Turning words into action

There are three components required to ensure promises become commitments. The components include a strong *Group focus*, *Accountability at the individual level* and *Patience from the leader*. The key is for all three components to be in place. Otherwise team members could be *floating*, feeling that agreeing to a set of behaviours is a *facade*, or becoming *frustrated*.

Table 14: The GAP Team Behavioural Model

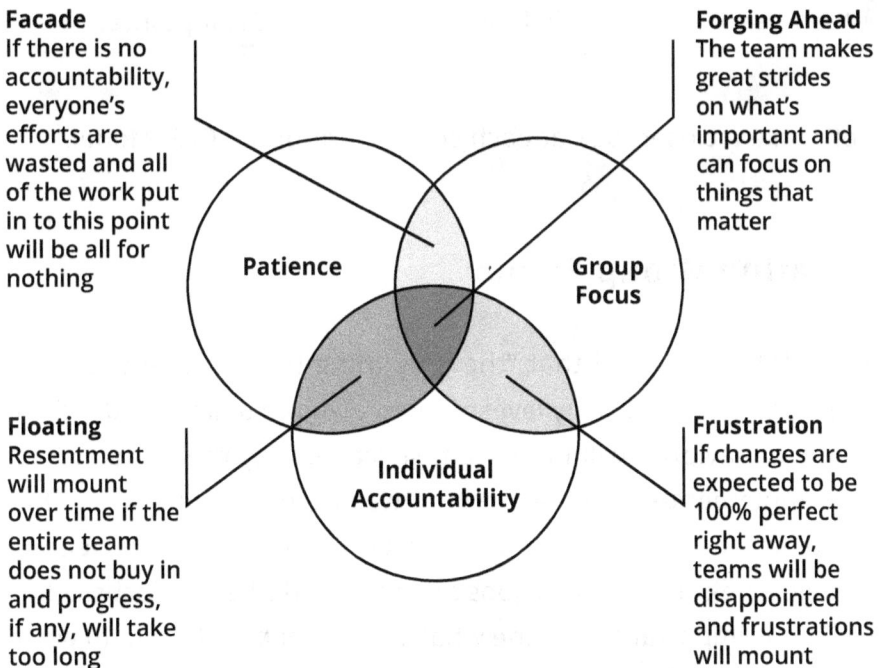

Facade
If there is no accountability, everyone's efforts are wasted and all of the work put in to this point will be all for nothing

Forging Ahead
The team makes great strides on what's important and can focus on things that matter

Patience

Group Focus

Floating
Resentment will mount over time if the entire team does not buy in and progress, if any, will take too long

Individual Accountability

Frustration
If changes are expected to be 100% perfect right away, teams will be disappointed and frustrations will mount

Table 15: What happens if one of the components of the GAP model is not in place

Floating	Façade	Frustration
A lack of **Group focus** results in individuals floating	A lack of individual **Accountability** makes people feel like agreeing to a set of behaviours was all a façade	A lack of **Patience** results in people getting frustrated
Inconsistent progress	No progress	Minimal progress
Lack of trust mounts towards the leader	Lack of trust mounts amongst each other	Trust builds for some, declines for others
'Confused'	'All for nothing'	'Disappointed'

Let's take a closer look at each component of the GAP Model.

Creating Group Focus

Steve Jobs once said that "the only thing that differentiates me from everyone else is my level of focus". Once a team has identified which behaviours will help them succeed, they then need to act and implement—as a team—what was agreed upon. To do this, the team needs to constantly focus on which behaviours need to change. Look at what Steve Jobs accomplished when he focussed on what was important. Imagine what a group of people can do when they decide to focus on what's really important to them.

So what's the key to maintaining focus on the new behaviours? Some suggest writing them up in a fancy PowerPoint presentation (which then gets filed five folders deep on a shared drive). Others say, 'Write them up on a wall!' (sporting teams are famous for this). Some teams I've seen have had their behaviours printed on cards they can carry around in their wallets. Not sure how many people will reach into their wallets to reference a team behaviour. I have also seen teams print out their behaviours and put them on tables in meeting rooms where people would reference them from time to time (this worked well).

Here are five easy ways to keep the group's focus on the agreed team behaviours:

1. **Leaders – recognise the right behaviours.** In schools, it's been demonstrated that for maximum effectiveness, teachers should give at least three times (five is ideal) more praise than corrective statements or discipline.[51] Recognise the right behaviours in front of a group, in a 1:1, in a handwritten note or even in email. As painful as emails can be, a simple one- or two-liner recognising alignment to a team behaviour can be incredibly powerful. Think about who you could cc into the email too. Maybe your boss or their boss.
2. **Colleagues and teammates – recognise the right behaviours.** It doesn't always have to be the boss highlighting the right behaviours. Anyone can do it. In a 1:1. In a team meeting. In a note or in an email (cc'ing the boss is good in this case too).
3. **Be specific about what is reinforced.** The what, the how, to whom. Be as specific as you can. Remember the story about the CEO who pulled $10 out of his pocket to pay for coffees instead of using his corporate credit card – hearing that specific story made others think about whether or not they needed to pull out their cards.

4. **Check in with the team regularly about how well they think they are going with the behaviours.** Heidi's team allocated five minutes in team meetings to check in to see how the group was going. As she said, "That helped us over time focus on particular behaviours that were less embedded than others." Asking the question then discussing it, getting team members to give the team a score between 0–10 and asking them what's contributing to the score (positively or negatively) is a simple way to keep the discussion going. If someone rates the team a 6, our initial tendency is to ask – what do you need to do to be a 10? Try this one. 'A six. That's good – what's been happening that's held you back from giving a lower score?' It will allow the team to recognise and reinforce what's going well, which creates momentum for further progress.

5. **Make the behaviours part of your team's regular dialogue.** Use the new language as a bridge from discomfort to safety when a team member witnesses a behaviour that is misaligned with what was agreed to. Heidi shared a story about how her team used the term 'Say it sooner' a number of times to help voice their disagreement. It sounded as simple as 'Guys, in the spirit of saying it sooner, I need to say I think we need to move quickly on this.' Or 'What do we need to say sooner before we finish off on this topic?'

Creating individual Accountability

Martina Navratilova knows a thing or two about accountability. As one of the greatest tennis players ever to play the game, if she wasn't accountable, she couldn't perform at the level she did. So when she talks about commitment and accountability, we could probably take a learning or two from her. She once said, "The difference between involvement and commitment is like ham and eggs. The chicken is involved; the pig is committed."

So let's talk pigs.

Once there is clarity about which behaviours are required for success and the team focusses on those behaviours, it's time to take action at the individual level. It's about each individual holding themselves accountable. This is where the talk for show, do for dough comes in.

Here are five ways to keep yourself accountable:

1. **Remind yourself why you agreed to this promise.** We often forget about the big picture, so remind yourself again why this is important to you.

2. **Give yourself a reward or something you will lose.** If you made a promise you are not 100% comfortable with, reward yourself when you fulfil it. The reward can be big or small, but recognising when you've done something good will help create momentum for the next opportunity. Or do the opposite – put something on the line that you will lose if you break your promise. Studies on loss aversion have suggested that losses are twice as powerful, psychologically, as gains.[52] I've seen one team put $10 in a jar at the beginning of the week and at the next Monday morning meeting, they self-judge whether they get their $10 back or not.

3. **Ask for feedback.** Ask your teammates how they think you are going with adhering to the promises. If you get positive feedback, great, keep going. If you get some feedback you weren't expecting, that's great too. You are looking for ways to be better, which is a great sign of holding yourself accountable.

4. **Change your environment.** Look around you. What's in your environment that is enabling an old habit or blocking a new habit. It could be something physical (for example, your phone). It could be the people you surround yourself with – does your group complain and gossip, or are they excited about fixing things?

5. **Check out James Clear's book.** Atomic Habits. Clear talks about starting with small habits, breaking habits into smaller chunks, habit stacking (pairing a new habit with an existing habit), and the 3 R's of habit change (reminder, routine and reward).

One of the promises that a team I was working with decided on was to 'Man Up', which related to the team's desire to address difficult discussions. Over time, the team grew really comfortable using the term 'Man Up'; it became a good reminder for team members to say, 'I have to man up and share something'. This allowed them to call out unproductive behaviours and keep each other accountable. However, the comfort levels didn't happen overnight. It took time, which leads us into the third component of the GAP model – Patience.

Leaders practicing Patience

You get the egg by hatching it, not by crushing it.

When I work with teams, I like to call my client a couple of days after a workshop to see how everyone's doing. Most times they say they can see change happening already. The most common change they report is about the language being used. Sometimes they say there is more swearing (remember, the research says this is good!). They also share that the promises are being discussed and incorporated in the team's everyday language. This makes me happy, and if Adrian is happy, then the world is great, right? The truth of the matter is, as much as this feedback makes me feel warm and fuzzy inside, I know it's going to be hard work to keep this new-found energy in the team going.

The reality of changing behaviours is that it takes time. The key is to be ok with this. It doesn't mean you have to accept the lack of change, but realise it takes time for a new habit to form. And the more patient you can be, the better it will be for your health and your team's performance.

Professor of Psychology Robert Emmons has proven patient people tend to experience less depression and fewer negative emotions, "perhaps because they can cope better with upsetting or stressful situations", as one 2016 article put it. He also reported that patient people were less likely to report health problems like headaches, ulcers, diarrhoea and pneumonia. When it comes to people achieving their goals, Professor Sarah A Schnitker demonstrated in 2012 that patient people "reported exerting more effort toward their goals than other people did," said the same article. "Those with interpersonal patience in particular made more progress toward their goals and were more satisfied when they achieved them (particularly if those goals were difficult) compared with less patient people."[53]

Apparently, the idea that it takes 21 days to change a habit has been debunked. Did you know the '21 days to make a habit permanent' concept is a case of 'heard it on the grapevine'? According to author James Clear, in the 1950s a plastic surgeon noticed it took around 21 days for his patients to become used to their new nose. The doctor also noticed it took him at least 21 days to form a new habit. *At least* 21 days. Over the years, the words 'at least' have fallen away from this theory because 21 days on its own is much more motivating, so the legend continues. Research (outside of one plastic surgeon's observations) would suggest it takes on average 66 days before a new behaviour becomes automatic. Health psychologist Phillippa Lally from the University College of London found it took anywhere from 18 days (almost 21!) to 254 days for new habits to be formed.[54] So, if you expect to be able to take action to create new team norms in 3 weeks, you may be disappointed. Well sort of.

There is one action you can take. And it's called patience. Author Joyce Meyer describes patience as "not the ability to wait. It's how we behave while we wait".

Think about it. When was the last time you decided to make a change? Drink less booze, exercise regularly, spend more time with the family, or stop eating ice cream after 8pm! You're excited, you're committed, you're going to make your life so much better. It's great isn't it. Then life gets in the way. One drink turns into nine, exercise gets pushed to the side because you were up late the night before. Or you choose to eat out of the ice cream container instead of from a small bowl. Next thing you know it's late, you've smashed out a two-litre container of Cookies and Cream and you know you'll pay the price the next morning on the toilet. How did this happen?

When looking to change team behaviours, it's the same. Your team identifies new behaviours. They make promises to each other. Everyone is excited and ready to move forward as one. You can feel the energy. Some people will adjust immediately. Some will take longer, and some simply won't change. Others will buy in and then slide back into old habits. Creating new habits is hard. Unlearning old habits is just as hard, if not more. Have you ever heard the phrase, 'It's like riding a bike, you never forget how'? Well what if you had to learn something new, something as simple as a new way to ride a bike?

Destin Sandlin from Smarter Every Day conducted an experiment to investigate how hard it is to unlearn something as simple as riding a bike. Destin and his buddies were mucking around one day and one of them decided to weld up a bike which turned left when you turned right and vice versa. The group figured with a little bit of practice, riding the bike would be no problem. How hard can it be? Once you learn how to ride a bike, you never forget, right? Well, not quite.

It took months of practice for Destin to rewire his brain, to essentially unlearn one skill and learn another. He describes it as "our brains trick[ing] us into thinking the same way". The more rigid our thinking, the more difficult it can become to change, even when we want to.[55]

Destin also concluded that knowledge on its own was not enough to change a habit. He suggests attitudes and skills play a big role in rewiring the brain, which usually comes after plenty of practice and trying to see things from numerous perspectives.

Depending on people's current behaviours (how their brain is wired), their background, previous experiences, attitude, skills and even age (Destin's son, aged six, learned to ride the backwards bike in weeks compared to the months it took his dad), some will adjust sooner than others.

So … what you are saying, Adrian, is be patient, right? Got it. So how patient do I need to be and what can I do to get this balance right? As we talked about in our discussion of the AAA approach earlier, if you accept, acknowledge and adjust, you'll find the right balance to ensure the right behaviours are implemented. Here's what I mean.

1. **Accept** people will not get it right all the time. Phillippa Lally's research on forming new habits also demonstrated that "missing one opportunity to perform the behavior did not materially affect the habit formation process". So, if people stuff up and

don't get it right immediately, it doesn't mean they won't ever get it or are not committed. As long as the mistake is acknowledged (good attitude) and there's a plan to get back on track sooner than later (skill development), then patience will pay off.

2. **Acknowledge** people's efforts. And their mistakes. Showing gratitude for people's efforts (and not just the outcomes) will continue to reinforce the right behaviours. Acknowledgement of the wrong behaviour is also important. Providing timely and productive feedback in the right environment is crucial to ensuring skills and expectations are clear. The key is how you provide the feedback. This is where the team behaviours and promises comes in – you can always refer back to the agreed behaviours to provide your feedback.

3. **Adjust** your focus. When I was one of three coaches for Saskatchewan's Canada Summer Games baseball team, we travelled across America and Canada in preparation for the tournament. We had 18 players between the ages of 17–21. Of those 18 players, two were a major pain in my side. I loved them, but they took up much more of my mental energy than required. Rob Cherepuschak, an educator and a great head coach who would later go on to lead one of his teams to a Western Major Baseball League championship, often reminded me that I could choose to focus on the pain-in-the-butt players or the 16 good ones. The same goes for being patient with your team while they adjust to new behaviours. If the effort is visible, mistakes are decreasing, and progress is being made, then choose to focus on and be grateful for what is going well.

Being patient allows you to focus on what you can control in a situation. Remember, it can take *on average* 66 days to develop a new habit. As Aristotle once said, "Patience is bitter, but its fruit is sweet."

Key Takeaways

☑ Behaviours can either block progress or enable it. The key is to minimise the bad ones and focus on the good ones that will make the biggest impact. Think big rocks.

☑ Get the team to identify what those key behaviours are. Talk about the impact they will have if the team lives by them and if they don't. Ask your team to promise to make those behaviours the foundation of how they work together.

☑ Leaders – you need to lead by example. Remember, people will look at you and use you as the barometer for what goes and what doesn't. Avoid jumping in the Bentley. And show patience.

Reflections

💡 What do you think are the key behaviours for your team that will help them really nail their performance for the next six months? What does your team think?

💡 What behaviours are you experiencing within your team that are contributing to success? Which behaviours are interfering with your team's potential?

💡 What role are you playing in the interfering behaviours?

SECTION 4

How to Create Higher Performing Teams Through Relationships

Creating clarity within the team is like using a map to get your team where you want to go. You've agreed on your destination, when you want to get there, who will do what to get you there, and what you'll need for the journey. That's the plan. To actually get to your destination, you now need the right resources: the right vehicle, petrol, tyres, some snacks, and if travelling in Australia, a good air conditioner. If in Saskatoon, most likely you'll need good heating.

When it comes to achieving meaningful progress at work with your team, the other biggest resource you'll need is the relationships between your team members. Richard Bowden (the CEO we made famous for paying for a coffee with his own money and not expensing it) was one of those corporate success stories who started out in an entry-level position and worked his way to the top where he was influential both domestically and globally. One of his sayings was "pace over perfection". Richard often spoke about how you can spend a lot of time developing the best strategy, but if you don't move with pace, the strategy can be all for nothing. Over the years I've seen many great plans on paper but when it comes to execution, very little progress is made. And often any progress that could be made is held up by poor relationships within teams.

Over the next four chapters, we will explore what makes strong relationships in the workplace. Whilst enjoying a lunch together or a bevvy or two after work is important, when it comes to strong relationships at work, there's a lot more to it. Managing and using conflict productively, giving and asking for feedback and creating an environment where people feel comfortable to be themselves are all critical. However, to do these things, you need trust. There are many ways to develop trust, and they all start with a connection. A strong connection makes learning, trusting and succeeding happen more quickly. And it makes things more fun.

CHAPTER 14

Creating relationships with connection and trust

Connection with someone is good so someone is looking out for me and I can look out for them.
~ YouTuber JB Amazing (who also happens to be my eldest son, Jack)

In order to be able to lead, you need to build trust. To build trust you need to have a connection.
~ Joe Maddon, Major League Baseball manager

I love Joe Maddon. In 1979, four years into his playing career, he decided to switch paths and started to scout, coach and manage in the minor leagues. Twenty-one years later he finally made it to the big leagues. For those not familiar with baseball, this would be the equivalent of being in an entry-level role for 21 years before getting a promotion. Instead of private planes, lavish hotels and fans clamouring for your attention, think numerous 14-hour bus rides over the course of six months, $20 food allowances and rooming with three other men in dodgy hotels.

Joe is famous for keeping things loose with his players throughout their 162-game season. He's been known to show up to training riding a camel. He has implemented American Legion Week, in which players are allowed to show up just one hour before the game, much like they did when playing minor sports as kids. Joe is also a fan of dress-up themes, which his players love, as do the folks at the airport when the team arrives. Whether it's crazy suits, cowboy hats or wacky hair dye themes, he knows how to mix things up.

Like many leaders, Joe believes trust is critical within a team. Patrick Lencioni, author of *The Five Dysfunctions of a Team*, suggests 'vulnerability trust' is the critical type of trust required in a team. As Lencioni says: "Trust is the confidence among team members that their peers' intentions are good, and there is no reason to be protective or careful around the group." This is vulnerability trust. "Teammates must be comfortable being vulnerable with one another," says Lencioni.

There are many different types and definitions of trust. Some say trust is based on what people have done in the past, which demonstrates credibility and reliability. Others say it's about demonstrating you are just as interested in the other person's outcomes as your own. Authors David Maister, Charles H Green and Robert M Galford suggest it's all the above in their Trust Equation.

Table 16: The Trust Equation

The Trust Equation

$$T = \frac{C\ (\text{Credibility}) + R\ (\text{Reliability}) + I\ (\text{Intimacy})}{S\ (\text{Self-Orientation})}$$

Credibility   = you have the skills and abilities to do what's needed

Reliability   = you do what you say you will do

Intimacy   = the safety or security you feel when entrusting someone with something

Self-orientation = what you believe the other person focusses on – their own interests or yours

This is very similar to what Lencioni refers to as vulnerability trust. As Lencioni says in *The Five Dysfunctions of a Team*, "Can I be myself, warts and all, knowing that they won't be used against me?"

Regardless of your definition of trust, Joe Maddon would suggest that whilst trust is critical, connection is the first step. And by connection, he means a personal connection. It's about getting to know something meaningful about the other person and being able to relate. Or it can be about finding something in common with someone, looking out for them, and sharing something important with them that says, 'Hey, you are important to me, and I think it's worth us spending some time together to see what we share in common.'

When a younger player joins his team, Joe spends a lot of time getting to know about their family. He also looks for ways to connect outside of baseball. He'll often take the time to teach the younger players about something he is quite passionate about – say, red wine. In a time when managers are encouraged not to get too close to their people (some argue it skews your ability to keep staff accountable), Joe bucks the trend. He knows trust is critical when it comes to working together, and that to establish trust, connection is paramount.

Think about some of the stronger relationships you have at work and some of the weaker ones. Which of the attributes of the characteristics below resonate with you? Consider the impact of having strong connections with your people and teams compared to having weaker ones.

Table 17: Impacts of different levels of connection with colleagues

Little Human Connection	IMPACTS ON	Strong Human Connection
Questioned	Mutual Respect	Shared
Hidden	Disagreement	Respected
Held back	Feelings	Shared
Drains	Energy	Gives
Protective	Own opinions	Curious
Formal	Formality	Informal
Hidden	Weird habits	Laughed at

Benefits of strong connections

Developing meaningful connections has many benefits. From a health perspective, if you are going to spend a large chunk of your time at work, it is healthy to develop strong social connections. Researchers Holt-Lunstad, Smith and Layton demonstrated that strong social connection can lead to a 50% increased chance of longevity.[56] Other research also suggests that social connection strengthens our immune system[57], helps us recover from disease faster, and may even lengthen our life.[58] Moreover, we know that people with strong social connections also have higher self-esteem, are more empathic to others, and are more trusting and cooperative; and as a consequence, others are more open to trusting and cooperating with them.[59]

Connection in action

I once worked with the senior customer service leadership team at Mystikal Financial,* a large financial services organisation. The team was responsible for leading several hundred people providing customer service over the phone across Australia and New Zealand.

Over the previous 12 months, there had been some changes in this leadership team. Three of the six team members had joined in the past year. Whilst each individual was performing at an acceptable level (they were meeting their individual KPIs), the manager, Roy, felt they were not truly working as a team. Information and best practices were not being shared. Progress was being made, but not at the rate they were capable of.

"It's like we've been in the storming phase for the last year," explained Roy. "Individually, they do a really good job. But there seems to be some underlying tensions that haven't been ironed out yet and I feel if we can get past these, we will have a much bigger impact. And selfishly, there will be fewer issues for me to sort out."

Storming for a year. Ooh, that sounds painful. Unresolved conflict. Increased internal competition. Cliques forming. Maybe some talking (and probably some swearing) about each other behind each other's backs. Sounds great, doesn't it? Not!

---

* Names of the company and individuals have been changed for the sake of maintaining privacy.

Over time, we realised storming was exactly what was going on. Even amongst a team of six, cliques had formed. And there were some serious trust issues, which their AB Team Dynamics Assessment identified. Yet when I presented the results back to the team and suggested there appeared to be trust issues, the response from the team was dead silence. You know that real awkward silence where after 5–10 seconds, someone usually pipes up with something for the sake of breaking the silence? Well, the silence continued. Until eventually, someone jumped in.

"Well to be honest, I have some serious trust issues within this team. There have been a couple of times where my trust has been broken and I don't feel I can trust some of the people in this room."

Boom! Jackpot, I was thinking. This type of courage, honesty and vulnerability is exactly what brings teams together. I'm not so sure the rest of the room was as excited as I was.

Nikki had broken the silence. Her words were the jolt the team needed. I guarantee everyone in the room was thinking, 'Shit, did I do something?' Another long silence ensued. You could see the team was uncomfortable.

Nikki's statement broke the ice and highlighted that despite the fact the team had been working together for over six months, there was very little connection between them. One person shared that when they were at work they just wanted to get the work done and that they behaved in a very different way than how they did at home. "I am like two very different people, and I'm fine with that."

Following that meeting, the team committed to catching up individually with Nikki to understand what had happened. For some of the team members, it was the first time they had ever had a one-on-one conversation with her. Remember Pentland's research finding that higher performing team members communicate with each other and not just the boss? This was a perfect example of this *not* happening and look where it landed the team.

So there it was, progress already being made simply by one person sharing how she felt within the team. Well done Nikki. But there was more work to be done. Connection doesn't happen overnight and with one conversation. One person had demonstrated vulnerability, but we needed it to be a team effort.

The next time we caught up, I took the team through a Map of Life exercise. I asked each team member to share how they have become who they are today. The stories we heard were amazing and impactful. Nikki shared some funny stories about her years in high school. She also shared the challenges of being a single mum. Kim, one of the younger members of the team, described a stage in her life where she became a stalker of an ex-boyfriend. Not quite the boiled bunnies-type of stalker, but 'I would wait outside of the gym in my car and follow him home'-type of stalker. The group loved this story. Another team member, Oliver, shared how, growing up, he had always sensed he was a little different than others and then when he was 28, he was diagnosed with Asperger's. He also shared how he had decided he'd had enough of a previous role in law enforcement role because he had been stabbed too many times (his words, I swear). Another member, Josh, really dropped his guard. When you hear "I've only told this to three people in the world" followed up by "I've had some pretty serious depression and anxiety issues in my life", you can't help but feel closer.

So creating a connection can bring people together. For this group, the impact of building stronger connections combined with identifying which behaviours would drive success built a foundation for improved team dynamics. When I completed follow-up surveys with the team, these were the levels of change:

Table 18: Impacts of improved relationships at Mystikal Financial

Team Dynamic Trait	Charge
1. Comfort levels in sharing personal challenges	↑ 150%
2. Confidence levels that others do not hold mistakes against each other	↑ 60%
3. Comfort levels in asking for help	↑ 39%
4. Confidence levels in giving feedback to each other	↑ 60%
5. Confidence levels in speaking out when they disagree	↑ 113%
6. Comfort levels in reaching out for support	↑ 100%

In addition to these results, the team also identified how they could leverage each team member's natural strengths. Take Oliver for example. Living with Asperger's no doubt presented him with certain challenges. When he shared this about himself, a penny dropped for some of the team. Some of the traits of people with Asperger's include being able to perceive errors that are not apparent to others, having a high attention to detail, being very direct, verbalising what's on their mind, and being comfortable telling the truth.

What great skills to have. A team member who can be honest, direct and to the point. Sounds like a great person to make quick decisions. Or proofread, or Red Team a strategy or new approach.

And let's look at Josh, who was based in a different country from most of his colleagues. As he said, "One of the things my anxiety impacts is my ability to deal with being pulled into last minute or unplanned meetings. I get sick to the stomach and it makes me very ineffective in that meeting. So where I can, I try to plan out my trips as much as I can with who I need to see."

When Josh spoke about his anxiety, he shared how it impacts his visits to the Australian office. One of his coping mechanisms was to send a Microsoft Excel schedule template for his trips to his colleagues so they could fill in the details of any meetings he would need to attend. Similar to Oliver, the team identified a natural—or at least heavily developed and refined—skill in Josh. Planning ahead is part of Josh's everyday life. Not just his work life, but his whole life, as it helps him cope with the challenges that come with his anxiety. If it was me, and the team needed some team planning, Josh would be the guy I would go to.

Sharing personal stories is a great way to bring a team closer, create a greater understanding of each other and start to develop a stronger connection.

Connection amongst the Tigers

More and more stories are starting to emerge about teams focussing on connecting. And it's not just in the corporate world.

Heading into the 2017 season, the Richmond Tigers of the Australian Football League had not won a premiership since 1980. Their diehard fans were desperate for a return to glory. Their head coach, Damien Hardwick, was said to be in year seven of his five-year plan. There were calls for his sacking after 2016. The club had to make changes.

One of the changes they introduced were the HHH sessions. Beginning in the pre-season, players would take turns sharing a *hardship*, *highlight* and *hero* of their lives. Coach Damien Hardwick thought the approach would help bring the team together.

And bring the team together it did. "It brought a sense of family, a sense of connection with each other," said Hardwick.[60] As AFL commentator Nathan Schmook noted, "The sessions created more conversations between players, coaches and staff, and deeper connections were made in the follow-up."[61]

Player Bachar Houli said, "All eyes and ears were open and I could see by looking around that their hearts were open as well. That's the connection we've built."[62]

That year—2017—was a special year for the Tigers. Not only did they become closer as a unit and build stronger connections. They also won their first premiership in 37 years. And two years later, they followed it up with a second. Players and coaches have attributed a lot of their success to the stronger connections they built. Opening up, being vulnerable to each other and connecting at a personal level helped the players and club become what they are today.

Barriers to connection

At work, there are natural and unnatural barriers that prevent connection from happening. Working in different locations and office set-ups, with team members with different personalities, and a lack of understanding about how to get the best out of those different personalities can prevent relationships from developing. However, with deliberate focus and an open-minded attitude, there are ways to overcome these barriers. Here are some ideas to help you and your team overcome some of these barriers.

Barrier 1: Distance
With more people working remotely, connecting as a team can be challenging. Making face-to-face meetings a priority where possible is a good first step. A group of Imperial Oil employees

from four different departments all based in the same Canadian city committed to a weekly routine of meeting every Monday morning at a local breakfast shop to kick off their week. There was no formal agenda, but without fail, everyone showed up. The discussions naturally gravitated toward work, what everyone was doing for the week and challenges that people were having. It was also a time to socialise, talk about the weekend and share a few laughs. It would have been too easy for some to say "I spend too much time driving to and from this meeting for this to be worth my while" but everyone made the commitment. They drove from different areas of the city to meet and as a result, were able to leverage each other's knowledge, connections and experiences.

If regular face-to-face is not possible, look to amplify what you can do with videoconference options. And actually use the video functionality. Seeing your team members via the video functionality allows you to pick up on some of those important social nuances that Sandy Pentland from MIT highlighted in his research. As the workforce becomes more comfortable with the technologies available for virtual catch-ups, be creative with how your teams connect. Have a go at virtual meetings, but also lunches, drinks and workshops.

One of my favourite ways to create some fun connection and overcome the distance barrier comes from Lucy Coggan, a senior marketing leader who has worked across government, health and care, and insurance industries. With team members living in Melbourne and Sydney, Lucy introduced Vino VC Wednesdays. Once a month, the team would pick a Wednesday afternoon, book VC rooms in Melbourne and Sydney and at 4:30pm have a wine together. On a somewhat more serious note, but still relaxed, Biogen Canada's Head of Commercial Hugo Bérardeau initiated a meeting for his team of regional managers, who came from all corners of Canada, to connect and enhance their leadership skills during the physical distancing restrictions of COVID-19. The team would meet monthly, with one team member sharing a leadership topic, article, podcast or video prior to the meeting. When the team caught up, they would share their thoughts, debate and challenge the chosen topic in a casual, late afternoon VC. What a great way to learn about each other, from each other, and evolve leaderships skills despite the 4,000 kilometres separating the team. Distance shmistance.

Barrier 2: Seating plans

Even when people are in the same office, distance can still be a challenge. There is an ongoing debate about the value of set seating plans versus more flexible arrangements such as hot seating. Some swear by hot seating, where you don't have a set seating plan. You show up to the office and grab a new spot every day. Whilst advocates of this approach claim people from different departments learn more about what's happening beyond their own patch of work, I'm not 100% convinced. Office design guru Jeff Pochepan shared his research findings that as much as 40% of an office's dedicated desk space sits unused on a given day.[63] Employees are on vacation, work a flex schedule, travel regularly or are stuck in back-to-back meetings. These empty desks are seen as an inefficient cost, therefore hot seating helps save costs. Ok, so hot desking can help save costs ... but what about the trade-off of not sitting with your team on a regular basis? Design development is maturing in this space, so people are able to sit in neighbourhoods where they're in close proximity to their teams. If you are heading down the flexible workspace path with unassigned desks, you need to put some good thought into finding the right design that allows natural connection to occur.

Whilst these ideas have worked for some in the past, it's important that leaders talk with their team as a whole as well as individual team members to figure out what will work for them to help them feel connected. The key is to ensure that it doesn't feel fake or contrived. For example, when teams work from home, some people may feel that calls—video or not—are an unwelcome interruption whereas others may feel isolated and unloved if such calls aren't scheduled. Understanding each person's individual needs and preferences for communicating is key.

Barrier 3: Open plan vs offices
Open plan workspaces are becoming the norm. Walls are being knocked down to remove communication barriers and to save costs. The theory is that fewer walls will increase communication and improve team morale by enabling more face-to-face time. Whilst this sounds like a good idea, you may want to reconsider. The *Journal of Environmental Psychology* reported that there was a trend in a recent study for workers in private offices to be more satisfied with ease of interaction than open plan workers.[64] Another study reported in *Harvard Business Review* found that workers who shifted to an open plan office space "spent 73 per cent less time in face-to-face interactions, while their use of email and instant messenger shot up by 67 per cent and 75 per cent respectively".[65]

So how can you manage connection when your team works across an open plan office, in cubicles, and enclosed offices?

First, ask each team member what their preference is. Do they mind the odd drop-in, 'Hey can I ask you something?' conversation? Or would they rather a quick note or message to give them a heads up you'd like to talk about something? International speaker, author and overall funny guy Colin D Ellis (who also happens to be one of the leading voices in project management) concluded in *The Project Book* that by any measure *everyone* is different. (Which was confirmed by a set of twins he questioned as part of his informal survey. "This was a relief for my statistical analysis," he noted wryly). Ellis also points out that the key to getting your people to do their best work is to align their environment with the right task. He suggests that regardless of the office set-up, there are four types of working environments required for teams. Quiet environments (to get work done), private environments (where private or group discussions need to take place), group environments (where people work on a problem together), and social environments (to build relationships or break up the monotony of tasks for a group).

The key takeaway from Ellis's point is this. Regardless of your office set-up, you need to find the way that works best for your *team*. Talk about it. Ask them questions. If the team finds the working space prevents them from having robust debates and agree these discussions are critical, then use another space (a meeting room, outside, a corner in the lunchroom). If workstations (quiet environments) are becoming too noisy, flag this as a group and establish some ways of working regarding these workspaces. Whilst discussions are a great way to connect, talking too much (and too loudly around others) can have the opposite effect. Even though we don't necessarily control our physical environment, we do control how we use it and can decide how to make the most out of it as a team.

Barrier 4: The boss's office
From a leadership perspective, the corner office with a view has always been a sign of prestige and power. But does a boss's office help or hinder?

Being around employees helps leaders develop better relationships with their team members. I have seen examples of leaders who are approachable regardless of whether they have an office or not. However, if leaders want to develop trust and deeper connections, and increase the chance that team members will share issues with them as soon as they occur, then using the office as a meeting room instead of a personal haven can help.

I often hear managers say they need an office so they can have private discussions without other team members overhearing. I must admit, I find this a little patronising. Yes, there may be some people-related discussions that need privacy. However, many people, regardless of their role, have what could be deemed sensitive discussions. Call centres have sensitive discussions with customers all the time. Others have sensitive discussions with their staff, suppliers, colleagues across the country (or on different floors), or with family. And somehow, they manage to have these discussions without having an office.

If you are worried about not being able to maintain focus or being interrupted too much, once again, I find this a little patronising. There are ways to manage this. Adopt a visual signal to indicate you'd prefer not to be interrupted (a little flag or headphones whether you have music on or not). Establish a designated quiet space or time of the day where you'd like to go uninterrupted. Be creative, and let your team know when you need to not be interrupted.

Barrier 5: Personalities
I am sure there are people you clash with. History has a long list. Michelangelo and Leonardo da Vinci. Rocky and Ivan Drago. The Yankees and the Red Sox. Collingwood Magpies and everyone. In these instances though, folks are competing against each other. Even though we might forget sometimes when we're at work that we're on the same team, it

doesn't mean we will always get along. Sometimes events arise that cause friction and sometimes it's simply due to a clash of personalities.

Personality tests can provide us with great insights into what drives people and why they behave the way they do. One of the more common personality profiling tools, the Myers-Briggs Type Indicator, focusses on Carl Jung's concept of introverts and extroverts. Some studies show that roughly 50% of people identify themselves as introverts and roughly the same as extroverts. Except for librarians. A study conducted in 1998 suggests that over 60% of librarians are introverts. The quiet, peaceful environment would be ideal for a true introvert. Yet other studies suggest two-thirds of the population are ambiverts (somewhere in the middle). The key takeaway is that when you are working with a group of people, they will all have different ways they like to work together and connect.

Talk to your team members about whether they resonate more with introverted tendencies or extroverted tendencies. When you understand how you all like to work, you'll have a much better chance of building stronger connections. Here are a few tips for connecting with introverts and extroverts:

Connecting with introverts:

- Respect their private time. They value it the most. Avoid dropping in on them or making out-of-the-blue phone calls.
- Mix in smaller, intimate team activities. Team dinners at someone's house instead of a loud, boisterous restaurant. Smaller team development and training sessions instead of in large groups.
- Avoid surprises. Surprise tasks, changes or meetings. Give them advance notice, plan ahead where you can. Remember, they are deep thinkers and their minds don't change direction easily.

- Give them a heads up on the topics or challenges you'll be discussing in team meetings and workshops ahead of time.
- Go to them with the bigger problems. Avoid small talk. They can do it, but they get much more out of talking about more meaningful topics.

Connecting with extroverts:

- Encourage their enthusiasm. Let them dive headfirst into a problem and see how many possibilities they can come up with.
- Listen. They like to talk things out. Let them go through their thought process without you interjecting.
- Avoid telling them what to do. Give them the challenge and let them go and explore.
- Don't shelter them from surprises – they can deal with them. Particularly thoughtful extroverts. Recognise them in front of a group when they are not expecting it.

Remember – not everyone falls 100% into the different buckets. But the more effort you put into understanding each other's personalities, the more likely you are to develop meaningful connections, which ultimately lead to greater levels of trust.

How to get the most out of all personalities in a group setting

Bryce G Hoffman, author of *Red Teaming*, shares several ideas when running workshops with teams for getting the best out of both introverts and extroverts, and ensuring people don't keep their thoughts to themselves. One idea is called 124All.

124All looks like this:

Step 1: Put a question to the team. It can be about a problem, an issue, a presentation, proposal or opportunity. Whatever it is you want the team to work on. 'What did you think of the proposal?' 'What would you do in this situation?' 'How would you handle this?' 'What could we do next?'

Ask them to reflect individually and write down their responses. Tell them how much time you'll give them (one minute is fine, or up to five minutes). Don't rush this, remember your introverts prefer deep thinking and your extroverts will come up with numerous ideas.

Step 2: Pair up and generate ideas together, referencing the thinking from the self-reflection. Again, outline how much time they will have. Two to five minutes will be fine.

Step 3: Move into groups of four. Follow the same approach as previously. Track what's the same and what's not.

Step 4: Bring everyone together and ask each group to share the one idea that stood out in their conversations. You can give everyone two minutes each, or allocate the entire group a set time, say five minutes. The timing of this exercise is up to you. I've done this with a group of 30 and completed it in 20 minutes. Another option to ensure your introverts have an opportunity to do their deep thinking is to send out the question ahead of time so those who want to can reflect on it beforehand.

How to create stronger connections with your people

Over my time as a leader, and team and executive coach, I have come across many different ways teams create strong connections within them. One thing to point out – some of these activities require a decent level of self-disclosure. If you want to get the most out of these exercises—and develop meaningful connections—you need to lead by example. You need to be prepared to share some of your most challenging times, some of your proudest times and some of your most embarrassing times. Regardless if you are the official 'leader', the impact you can make on your team by being open, honest and real is broad. It will draw people closer to you and build a different level of trust, and people will be much more open to helping you when you need it.

Check in with your team
This might sound like common sense, but I am continually surprised when outcomes from workshops include, 'Ask everyone how they are doing before talking work at meetings'. It's not as obvious as I thought so look to start team meetings or a 1:1 with, 'How are you feeling today?' followed up by, 'Tell me more about that'. And then just listen. Giving folks a chance to share what's important to them is a great way to build connection.

Create shared experiences
Creating shared experiences allows you to connect socially and professionally. Shared experiences also allow you to reference back to the experience in future discussions. Go to a pre-work talk or networking event as a group. Team up and listen to calls in a call centre. Visit customers together. Drop into head office, a distribution centre, a supplier, a partner together. Spend time with the frontline or a senior leader together.

Or be a customer together. Literally. ThedaCare, a five-hospital system in Wisconsin, did exactly this. A team of employees became patients at the hospital as preparation for redesigning its critical service delivery system. Not only can sharing experiences increase the connection amongst team members, it can drive better results too. The changes the team members recommended contributed to improvements in safety, efficiency and effectiveness.[66]

Learn together
This can be formally through paid or free courses. Paid courses are typically away from the office, where people are more likely to be relaxed and social. If paid courses are not an option, look at doing a free online course or webinar together. Grab a meeting room and jump in front of a screen together. Informal learning is also beneficial and can bring people closer. Firefighters regularly debrief on their way back from being called out. They talk about what went well, what didn't and what to look out for next time. Chris Myers studied flight medical teams at university hospitals and found that they regularly used lunch breaks to find each other and share case-based stories, which was vital for learning about new diagnoses and techniques. You can also look to teach each other. You don't need to be a teacher to share information. You'd be amazed at what you can research and teach each other. Learning something with someone or as a team is a great way to connect and have some fun at the same time.

Share your passion
Joe Maddon, my beloved baseball manager guru, loves wine. He would teach his young players about it. He had different kinds of club awards that featured wines. Players would bring him bottles, trying to impress him with how much they had learned. Even when

he was let go by the Cubs in 2019, he sat down with his boss to have the discussion over a bottle of red ("Several!" interjected Joe when they announced his departure to the media).

What are you passionate about? What do you love that you could share with your team? You don't have to be the leader to share your passion either. Sharing your passion is a great way to drop your guard, welcome people into your world and develop a strong bond and sense of trust.

Volunteer together

A risk and compliance leader organised for her team to volunteer at one of their aged care homes. Not only did they get a better understanding of what it's like to work at an aged care home, they also shared memories of their grandparents. There was laughter and tears, all creating human connection.

Another leader encouraged their team to pick a charity to provide their technical services to for a day. The team developed a strategy for the charity and connected them to other key partners who could help in the execution of the strategy. The team identified this as one of the highlights of the year.

Walk in each other's shoes

Imagine if someone came to you and said, 'I'd love to learn from you and understand what it's actually like to take on the challenges you do. Would you mind if I spent some time shadowing you?' It could be for a couple of hours, a half day or full day. I love this one. Imagine the impact if a manager did that with one of their people. Or someone who reports into your peer, an IT manager with a customer service manager, or an external partner or supplier with their partner/purchaser.

You can do this as a one-off, monthly, quarterly – there is no set formula but getting a taste of what the other person deals with will bring you closer.

In an attempt to improve the relationships between the sales and marketing teams, one of the outputs of a workshop I ran for a financial services organisation was a commitment from the entire marketing team to spend half a day in the field with a sales rep within two months of the workshop. This allowed the marketing team to gain invaluable insights into the challenges the sales reps faced, it brought them closer to the customer, and gave them a chance to share their challenges and ideas with folks on the frontline.

Share stories

Ask yourself, 'How have you become the person you are?' Answer this question verbally, with photos or a drawing. Include challenges, proud moments, influential people and times. Talk about your childhood, your parents and what you loved doing. The key is to really open up and be vulnerable. I suggest letting people share their story in 10 minutes; it's long enough to garner some meaningful insights, and short enough for those who are not comfortable speaking in front of others.

This one is courtesy of John Rizzo, one of my previous managers. When kicking off one of our team offsites, John asked each person to share a photo from high school and talk about what we were like back then. High school for some was an awkward moment in life, while for others was full of cherished memories. Sharing these experiences with your team is an opportunity to be vulnerable, to provide a deeper insight into who you are and to create stronger bonds. Regardless of what is shared, the hairstyles and clothing from these times are sure to bring about a few laughs.

Try Richmond's HHH – hero, hardship and highlight sharing. Finish regularly scheduled meetings with someone taking 10 minutes to share their HHH.

Pick one of your favourite children's books. Share why the book resonates with you, which character most aligns with your personality and who introduced the book to you.

Share a photo of what you believe represents leadership and explain why. It could be a person or an object. A quote, a song or a movie.

Other ideas

Ask for feedback. I like to call feedback 'insights'. Seek insights into the impact you are making. Your colleagues, peers, team and executive will respect your attempt to get better. And they will remember you for it. We can all remember someone who gave us a piece of feedback that made a real difference for us, whether we agreed with it at the time or not.

Express gratitude. With a handwritten note or card. Even an email or text. Or a voicemail. If your colleague doesn't answer their phone, leave a message (I suspect they will listen to it more than once). You can even create a short video on your phone and send it to them. Share it on a weekend when they are not expecting it. Or best of all … grab two chairs, get face-to-face, look them in their eyes, and tell them why you are grateful to have them in your life. I know people will roll their eyes at this one, but the impact of this can be huge professionally and personally.

Create a team ritual around making time together. Monthly lunches or weekly coffee runs together. Two senior leaders at one firm used to make it a priority to catch up every three weeks and they did so by walking to one of the local specialty chocolate shops near the office. They took turns buying each other a treat (it cost each person $48 for the whole year), discussed work challenges and bounced ideas off each other. It became a routine they both looked forward to and the conversations during those walks led to their teams working closer together. It didn't mean they always worked perfectly, but over time it helped the leaders become much more open about where they saw problems arising which allowed them to find resolutions more quickly.

Key Takeaways

☑ Trust is critical to the success of any team. Creating a connection is a great first step to establishing trust.

☑ Being vulnerable, honest and dropping your guard helps make connection happen sooner rather than later.

☑ There are many barriers in today's workforce to creating connections amongst team members. To ensure your team has a strong connection, be deliberate about ensuring there are opportunities for them to make connections.

Reflections

💡 Who do you have a strong connection with at work? How come? What insights can you apply from that experience to your team now?

💡 Who do you have a less than ideal connection within your team? What's one thing you could do to initiate to a stronger connection?

💡 Ask this question at your next team meeting: 'Do you think teams perform better if team members like each other?' See what kind of answers you get.

CHAPTER 15

Creating relationships with psychological safety

safety: secure from threat of danger, harm, or loss; or successful at getting to a base in baseball without being put out.

~ Merriam-Webster Dictionary

When we're children, many fond memories are created through important milestones. Our first word, first step, first poo on the toilet,* first day of school, first kiss ... and the list goes on. For some perhaps odd reason, I can also remember the first time setting up my own bank account back in Saskatoon. Mom brought me to Scotiabank at the back of the Avalon Shopping Plaza and I can vividly remember excitedly walking out with my bank booklet and cheque book.

Many Australians were introduced to this experience through a program called Dollarmites, an initiative developed by the Commonwealth Bank of Australia (CBA) and which has run since 1931. This junior saver program made it easier for kids to make deposits than walking to the Scotiabank – kids were able to make deposits into their accounts from school. It's a pretty clever idea – teaching kids to save and associate banking with the CBA at an early

---

* As a parent, I think we are more excited about this one as the thought of diapers being a distant memory is greatly anticipated.

age. My kids went through this experience – upon signing up, they received a plastic piggy bank and regular newsletters in the post, and most importantly for the bank, developed the regular habit of making deposits at school. Sounds like a pretty good program.

Until 2018. At this time, it was revealed to the public that accounts were being fraudulently manipulated to ensure bank staff hit their KPIs and achieved their bonuses. Fortunately, customers weren't actually losing any money. In fact, some customers were given money. If there were no deposits within 30 days of the account being set up, it wouldn't technically qualify as a new account – and not count towards employees' targets. So bank employees would deposit small amounts—less than a dollar—to ensure the new account was activated and counted towards their targets.[67]

Stories like this are not uncommon. We saw earlier how the Victoria Police falsified breath tests. After the Space Shuttle Columbia tragedy in 2003 which resulted in the deaths of seven crew members, it was discovered there were apparently eight missed opportunities to potentially prevent the accident. A full review conducted in 2008 was highly critical of the culture within NASA that meant problems were ignored and shortcuts were allowed on other safety issues.[68]

I am sure you can think of your own situations where something has happened, you questioned whether you should say something or not ... and ultimately chose not to speak up. Why? Most likely because of fear. Franklin Roosevelt suggested "The only thing we have to fear is fear itself." Yet at work, there are times when we have feared being looked down upon. Of being painted with the 'troublemaker' brush. Of not being in the boss's good books. Of losing our job. Or worse yet, of being hurt – emotionally or even physically.

Over my time in the corporate world, holding back my thoughts wasn't as dire as the NASA environment. It wasn't life or death.

However, keeping quiet, not sharing your thoughts, your insights or opinions can negatively impact the outcomes of the work you and your team undertake.

In 2017, the Australian Workplace Psychological Safety Survey canvassed 1,176 Australian employees and found that only 23% of lower income-earning frontline employees felt their workplace was 'psychologically safe' to take a risk, compared to 45% of workers on significantly higher incomes. Regardless of income, that's more than half of people at work feeling they will be rejected for being different, or who aren't comfortable asking for help, or who feel mistakes will be held against them. Perhaps that's why folks at the Commonwealth Bank didn't say anything about fudging the kids' bank accounts. That's what Australian Finance Sector Union president Louise Arnfield thought. As reported in the *Sydney Morning Herald*, she said that "union members had been calling out the risks of systemic practices and bonus structures that put profit before all else – 'a culture where speaking up was often a dangerous thing to do'".[69]

Maybe that's why people at Volkswagen were also too scared. Why didn't anyone tell senior management about failed emission tests? Four years on from the initial revelations, VW apparently had paid more than €27 billion to settle investor and consumer lawsuits as well as regulatory fines and remedies to resolve the issues.[70] Ouch. Whilst it wasn't seven lives that were impacted, 27 big ones is a steep price to pay for not speaking up.

What is psychological safety?

According to Dr Amy Edmondson, the Novartis Professor of Leadership and Management at Harvard Business School, psychological safety plays a critical role in how teams perform and learn. I'd suggest it also impacts what gets said and what doesn't. Dr E coined the term 'psychological safety' and concluded "in psychologically safe environments, people believe that if they make a mistake, others will not penalize or think less of them for it. They also believe that others will not resent or penalize them for asking for help, information or feedback. This belief fosters the confidence to take the risks and thereby to gain from the associated benefits of learning."[71]

Proven benefits of psychologically safe teams

Being in a psychologically safe team is like knowing the water is warm in a pool before you jump in. If you know it ahead of time, no time is wasted – you jump in right away. If you're not sure, you'll dip your toe, slowly get in and decide if it's worth staying in or not. If the water is freezing, some won't jump in at all (that's me). In a team, it's the same. There are times when you'll hold back, other times when you'll move cautiously forward. And other times when you'll jump right in, keep moving forward and make progress like you wouldn't believe.

Research has shown that in safe environments, employee engagement increases[72], team innovation is better[73], teams learn more from their mistakes[74], and are more likely to develop successful processes.[75]

For reasons like this, we are starting to see more organisations put more focus on creating environments where people can share their mistakes, provide feedback up and down the chain, and feel safer to do or say what they think.

How does psychological safety look? Pixar Animation Studios, creators of critically acclaimed films including *Toy Story*, *Cars* and *Finding Nemo*, create psychological safety for their teams by assuming their films are no good at first. Imagine that – handing in your report, recommendation or proposal to your boss and saying, 'This isn't any good, hope you like it'. As Pixar co-founder Ed Catmull says, they plan to go from "suck to not-suck". And how do they do it? They've created something called the 'Braintrust'. The Braintrust works with the mindset that every time feedback is shared, it's given in the service of a common goal: to support and help each other as they try to make better movies. With that in mind, the Braintrust is a group of people who are experts in storytelling who work closely with the directors. The storyteller experts share problems they see in the director's perspective of the story being told. They don't provide solutions, they simply identify problems and leave the fixing to the directors.

Over at Google, some teams kick off every meeting by sharing a risk taken in the previous week. This one action alone improved psychological safety ratings by 6% and 10% on structure and clarity ratings.[76]

Daniel Coyle, author of *Culture Code*, shares a story about his research into US Navy SEAL teams. After every training run and every mission, the teams would undertake an AAR – After Action Review. They asked themselves three questions: what went well, what didn't and what would they do differently next time. Because it's a regular exercise and considered to be a learning experience, team members feel much more confident to tell the truth. "Those meetings are hard because people are pointing out flaws and being open about weaknesses," Coyle says, "but it is by far the most important thing a group can do together."

Team Safety Zones

Thinking about CBA, NASA or VW – many people had the option to speak up, share their thoughts, or shut up. Over time, some may have even tried all three. This is what can happen depending on which safety zone you are in at work. For teams to increase the likelihood of being more effective, I like to help them move away from what I call the Danger Zone, through the Defensive Zone and towards the Safety Zone as much as possible.

Table 19: Team Safety Zones effectiveness

Team Zones	What Teams Do	Effectiveness
Safety Zone	Speak up	20x
Defensive Zone	Selectively share	5x
Danger Zone	Shut up	1x

I've identified the *Safety Zone* as the space teams occupy when they feel they can share anything within the team. If they disagree, have something to add or are concerned about a decision, they will speak up. They will admit a mistake and look to learn—instead of blame—from others' mistakes. They do so because they believe they won't be punished or frowned upon. Some leaders suggest teams in the Safety Zone are 20 times more productive than teams that are in the Danger Zone.

The *Defensive Zone* refers to teams that aren't 100% comfortable speaking up with everyone about everything. They will sometimes share their thoughts, ask for help or give feedback. At best, they will share information when it really matters to them and when they believe there is little chance of any negative impacts for themselves. Worst-case scenario, they will share with some—in the form of gossip—but not do anything to rectify the situation.

The *Danger Zone* (cue the Kenny Loggins hit from the 1986 box office hit *Top Gun*) refers to teams that will not voice their disagreement to anyone. Team members are micromanaged, information is not widely shared, individuals feel like they can't say no and if they do, they are gone. Job security is a regular concern. Credit is rarely shared (although in these teams, there isn't much to celebrate). A workplace like this makes people too afraid to contribute their thoughts and experiences. They shut up in meetings, and rarely participate in discussions or take risks in their work because any misstep could be used to harm their credibility and damage their standing in the organisation.

Using the Team Safety Zone

Team Safety Zones are good tools to identify what's working and what's not within a team. In one of my workshops, I took a group of senior leaders through an exercise where they identified the impacts of being in different safety zones on a number of important issues. What they came up with was a checklist to see how safe people feel in teams. If they experienced anything that fell under the Defensive or Danger Zones, we then unpacked why and what would need to happen in the future to move closer to the Safety Zone.

Table 20: What happens in the different zones

What happens with ...	Safety Zone	Defensive Zone	Danger Zone
Mistakes	Shared with the team (and leader)	Shared with few (cautiously if at all with the leader)	Hidden
Receiving feedback	Grateful and seen as a growth opportunity	Impact depends on who it's from	Taken personally
Giving feedback	Factual and given to improve	Some given, some withheld	Avoided
Authenticity	Can be yourself	Switch back and forth	Masked
Confidence	High	Roller coaster	Low
Risk taking	Comfortable	Only if others approve	Last resort
Imposter syndrome	Presence is minimised	Presence comes and goes	Constant presence
Problems	Shared with the team	Shared with some, hidden from others	Hidden
Personal thoughts	Focussed	Back and forth	Distracted
Job security	No thoughts about	Thoughts creep in	Daily thought

Other triggers to suggest the team may not feel psychologically safe with each other include:

- *Everyone is always agreeing with each other.* If everyone is just nodding their heads day in and day out, chances are they are simply nodding to be nice. If teams feel 100% comfortable with each other, they will be able to disagree (in a productive way of course), which we will touch on later in Chapter 17.
- *Everyone knows all the answers all the time.* If the words 'I don't know' are rarely used in front of the group, I'd be asking why. Yes, it takes big kahunas to admit you don't know something in front of your peers. But in an environment where you feel everyone has your back, saying these three words will foster feelings of support and safety versus feelings of stupidity and shielding.
- *Everyone is right all the time.* We are human and we all make mistakes. In a psychologically safe environment, the words 'I was wrong' will be shared regularly.
- *Colleagues swearing about each other – behind their backs.* Are people coming to you to dump their problems about a teammate? Or complaining about someone instead of talking to that someone? If so, then what can you do to create an environment where people can talk about their challenges face-to-face, adult to adult? Tough one ... yes. Is there an answer ... yes. Hang tight, we'll address this one soon.

Three ways to build psychological safety

When I first started supporting leaders in the capacity of a facilitator and coach, I was fortunate enough to be introduced to a gentleman by the name of Mr Cam Carter (thanks Margie for the intro). Mr Carter, who has a long and storied career in the advertising and media industry which included being MD of McCann Erickson as well as Leo Burnett across 27+ years, said to me once: "There is something fascinating about the number three. All good things come in threes. The Good, the Bad and the Ugly. The Father, the Son and the Holy Ghost. The Three Little Pigs. Paper, rock, scissors." And of course—my favourite—the three voices in *Field of Dreams*: "If you build it, he will come/ease his pain/go the distance."

Well, building psychological safety is no different. If you take the time to build it, it will come. It will definitely come. So in honour of Mr Carter, here are three ways to put deliberate focus on creating an environment where people feel safe.

Three things leaders can do to create psychological safety

1. **Admit and share when you've been wrong.** Whether you realise it or not, the shadow of your leadership is powerful. Brené Brown says, "Being vulnerable is what makes you beautiful." I also like to say it shows that you are human and relatable. The three words 'I was wrong' coming from your mouth allows people to be comfortable with their own mistakes. A senior executive once told me she did this by not being fixated with being right: "Willing to be wrong is key to my team's success. And it has to start with me." She has gotten into the habit of saying 'I was wrong' on a regular basis, four to five times a day. In front of her people and in front of her boss. The outcome? The team is much more comfortable sharing mistakes. They've avoided future mistakes costing them time and money by sharing and learning from each other's mistakes.

2. **Observe your reactions – verbally and physically.** When someone shares an opinion, an outcome (good or bad) or an omission, what do you say and how do you look? What are your patterns of response? How you respond will determine the level of safety your team will feel and determines how much sharing they will do next time. Observe what you say. What are the words that come out of your mouth? Are they, 'Tell me more', 'What's the take-out from this?' or 'What could we do differently next time?' Or is it, 'Why didn't you do ...', 'Why hasn't this progressed sooner?' or a statement, 'You just aren't getting it'.

   Physically, what does your face do? What is your body language? Do you make one of those patronising, face scrunched up, insincere smiles combined with 'I hear what you are saying but ...'? Or is it nodding, maybe taking notes, with a curious look on your face?

   If you aren't sure, next time you are with the team, ask someone to look out for these expressions and gestures and see what they report. Or think about what you can record – visually or audibly. Some professional sports coaches mic themselves up during a game or training session so they can understand what they sound like and which words they use regularly. Others will have the video or audio transcribed to check what they are saying and identify trends so they can ensure they are communicating in a way that is productive and safe.

3. **Ask for feedback.** Avoid waiting for it. Get on the front foot and ask for it. What is it about you that is working for people? What isn't? Be curious. And don't stop there. Ask, listen and explore. Think ALE (ask, listen, explore). You'll be amazed at the impact these conversations will have on you and the people around you. A word of advice on this one if I may. When exploring use questions like 'Tell me more about that', 'What else?' and 'Can

you share an example of when I did that toward you?' Avoid disagreeing or defending your version of the story. That would be ALED and ALED-ing is not good. If you struggle with this, think of two ALEs (ask, listen, explore, ask, listen, explore).

Three things team members can do to create psychological safety

When it comes to what your team can do to create a safe environment, it's amazing how much difference the fundamentals can make.

1. **Be present.** I'm trying to avoid telling you what to do in this case, but, what the hell, I'll tell you anyways. Put the bloody phone/laptop/tablet/whatever technology gadget that's taking your eyes, ears and thoughts away from whoever is speaking away. This will increase the levels of interaction and demonstrate that everyone is paying attention. It blows me away sometimes when I present to executives that their laptops are open and it's obvious people are reading emails and not listening. Perhaps that's an assumption on my part (or maybe a reflection of my presentation), but when they're looking at their devices the message they're communicating is that what I have to say is not important. Which makes me wonder whether what I have to say is important or not, which could have serious consequences down the track (I wonder if anyone from NASA ever felt this way?). It also makes me wonder about their business sense if they're paying me to be there then not paying attention. A financial services customer service team that I worked with decided to ban technology from team meetings. It was a productive step. Trust levels rose by 62%. Psychological safety levels went up by 83%. Boom!

2. **Let each other finish talking.** Avoid speaking over the top of each other. Seems so simple, yes? But it does not happen all the time. Yes, when it's emotional, the fight-or-flight (often masked as passion) system will kick in. However, that doesn't make it right. I was at an introduction meeting with a potential client and her manager, and in the 30 minutes I spent with them, I counted five times when they cut each other off to get their point across to each other (the meeting was to find out more about me, but I think I learned more about them and what it was like to work with them). Needless to say, my potential client lamented the fact she didn't feel valued, trusted or respected. It wasn't long before she left. Conflict can be good – but let's remember some of the manners our parents taught us.

3. **Ban the blame game.** Whether it's amongst your team or across your team and another department. It is unproductive, amplifies frustrations and negativity, and creates an acceptance of finger-pointing rather than solution-finding. Blame often turns into gossip and gossip is a team-breaker, so cut that crap out too.

Three words everyone can use

Here is a list of easy to remember three-word sentences you can use to help foster safety amongst your group.

I was wrong.
You were right.
I am sorry.

I don't know.
Tell me more.
Help me understand.

Please go on.

Let's explore that. (This one works especially well when delivered with sincere enthusiasm.)

Can I help?

Are you ok?

I believe you.

You got this.

Team Exercise: Creating the blueprint of safety

Here's a great activity to do with your team to get them thinking about their experiences with psychological safety in the workplace and help improve the safety in your team. You can do this activity as a group or ask everyone to do it on their own (recording their answers in a notebook), then come to a meeting to share their thoughts with the group.

- Think about a specific situation when you felt psychologically unsafe at work. What happened to make you feel this way? Write down the specific details.
- Think about a situation when you felt psychologically safe at work. What specific actions contributed to this feeling?
- Group all the responses into themes. Choose one or two themes where the team thinks they could be better. As German poet Johann Wolfgang von Goethe wrote, "Knowing is not enough; we must apply. Being willing is not enough; we must do it." Come up with two team actions (things the team or each individual could do) to improve in the chosen area and revisit the impacts of those actions within six weeks.

Key Takeaways

☑ Psychological safety is about creating an environment where people can ask for help, make mistakes and share opinions without worrying about being resented or punished. Research confirms it improves how teams work, and increases team members' confidence to take risks, learn and drive better results.

☑ There are three zones of psychological safety to consider: the Safety Zone, the Defensive Zone and the Danger Zone. Depending on which zone people are in, they will speak up, share with a select few, or shut up.

☑ Be deliberate about creating safety. If you build it, it will come.

Reflections

💡 With whom and about which topics do you shut up, speak up or selectively share? What might be driving this?

💡 Which topics cause your team to shut up, speak up or selectively share?

💡 Which three-word sentence could you use more this week to create a safer environment for your team?

A final thought on establishing safety within the team

Talking about creating safety within the team is one thing, encouraging it to happen is another. How many times have you heard a leader—or yourself—say you want the team to be a place of trust and safety? I've heard it many times in many different settings. When I felt safe in an environment, what ultimately made it safe were my experiences with the people in my team. In situations where I would share my thoughts, I would pick up on clues that would tell me if I should go on or not. It could be as straightforward as a follow up enquiry, a nod of the head, a lack of eye-rolling or hands thrown up. Or even something as subtle as the widening of the pupils (the more excited people are, the larger their pupils get). So let's be very clear here. You can talk all you want about safety within a team, however if the responses—subtle or not—by the team do not say 'Thanks for sharing' or 'Tell me more', then you could find yourself sitting in the Defensive or Danger Zones despite best intentions. And if this is the case, our next topic could be the key to getting back into that Safety Zone. And that topic is feedback.

CHAPTER 16

Creating relationships with feedback

The year 1976 was a big one. Apple was formed by the two Steves. NASA unveiled the first space shuttle, the Enterprise. Sylvester Stallone rose to fame with the release of *Rocky*. And I was just a twinkle in my parents' eyes.

For Larry Mullen Jr, 1976 was a pretty exciting year too. At 14, his desire to start a band was kickstarted by the arrival of a new drum set. With a handwritten poster shared on the notice board at his high school in Clontarf, a suburb in Dublin, Ireland, Larry successfully recruited six others to join the Larry Mullen Band. He quickly realised that leading was a little challenging. Two of the recruits left quite quickly (after the first jam session), one of the recruits—Paul Hewson—wanted to play guitar but couldn't play that well. And it didn't take long for the name 'Larry Mullen Band' to be replaced with 'Feedback'.

Encouraged by one of their teachers, the boys entered a talent show at their high school. This is where the story gets a little murky – some say the boys won the talent show, some say they didn't but were called out for an encore. Regardless of the outcome of the talent show, the band received feedback that the performance was a little messy, that they seemed ill-prepared and their timing was off.

The boys took on the feedback, kept working on their timing and evolved. Eventually they made it to London where they aspired to sign on with RSO Records. Unfortunately, they were knocked back but continued on.

Thankfully they did. They took on the feedback, the knock on the chin and eventually changed their name one more time. To U2. In 1980, Island Records snatched them up and Paul Hewson, known as Bono, and David Evans, known as the Edge, were on their way to selling over 170 million records worldwide, grossing US$1.7 billion in ticket sales from 1990–2016, winning 22 of 46 Grammy nominations and being inducted into the Rock and Roll Hall of Fame. Not bad for a group that was told their timing was off and they sounded messy.

In addition to the band's original name (Feedback) aligning so well with the theme of this chapter, U2's rise is a great example of how giving, receiving and responding to feedback can help create dream teams and drive success.

A 2009 Gallup study showed that 98% of employees fail to be engaged when managers give little or no feedback. And if there's little engagement at an individual level, it's going to be pretty hard to have it at a team level, which is quickly going to start impacting business performance. In 2012 Gallup released the findings from research across nearly 50,000 work units from 34 countries which showed that companies that score in the top 50th percentile for employee engagement have double the odds of success of those in the bottom half. In addition, those workplaces in the 99th percentile of engagement have four times the success rate of those at the first percentile. Four times. That's massive.

That being said, feedback can also do a lot of harm. Research published by the American Psychological Association showed that feedback only improves performance about one-third of the time, while actually making it *worse* one-third of the time.[77]

So the question becomes – is feedback a good thing for teams or a bad thing?

Well, according to an article published in the *Harvard Business Review* in 2014, 94% of feedback recipients felt corrective feedback improves performance *when it is presented well*. And employees want it. Gallup also reported that 65% of employees want *more* feedback.

And for all of you leaders out there, those leaders who ask for feedback are perceived more positively than those who are simply good at providing it.

So for all of you 'just get to the point' types – here it is:

- Employee engagement is critical to success.
- Feedback is key to employee engagement – as long as it's delivered the right way. If not, it does more harm than good.
- People want more feedback.
- It's a good idea to ask for feedback rather than wait for it to arrive.

Of all these points, the most important—and challenging—one to keep front of mind is that feedback can be productive *when delivered the right way*. Gallup researchers Nate Dvorak and Ben Wigert shared the following insights based on some of their research:

When most organizations had hierarchical, top-down, command-and-control structures as their primary decision-making method, feedback was paramount. Information mostly needed to cascade downward in an organization, and the primary role of managers was to hold people accountable.

Today, as leaders know, the workplace is radically different. Modern organizations are more decentralized, matrixed and

190

agile. Employees have greater autonomy and are required to be creative in how work gets done.

This means managers can't just give employees feedback about what they did "right" or "wrong." They must listen, ask questions, gain context and create a two-way dialogue.[78]

The boys go on to say feedback needs to be replaced with coaching conversations and focussed on the future. Whatever words you want to use—whether it be coaching conversations, feedback, corrective conversations, feedforward—one thing is for certain. Teams that can help each other provide and receive feedback well will succeed, grow and innovate.

Why it's hard

How many people love to use these six words, 'Can I give you some feedback?'

I'm not sure who cringes more when these words are spoken – the person saying them or the person hearing them. A study at the NeuroLeadership Institute in New York has demonstrated we become just as anxious when asked to give feedback as when asked to receive it.[79] Giving and receiving feedback is like Metallica playing with the San Francisco Symphony. Initially it's not natural and doesn't feel right. But if we give it a chance, the better it can sound.

Listening to feedback, though, is not easy initially. Physically and emotionally, feedback can hurt. The good thing is, it's not really our fault.

Peter Gray, a renowned psychologist at Boston College, suggests our brains respond to feedback as a social threat. Like the social threat of exclusion that we may have experienced in the playground.

Or like our Paleolithic ancestors who relied on groups to survive. If you weren't part of a pack, you most likely wouldn't survive.

With all threats, our bodies, emotions and brains respond to protect us. Think about the last time someone said to you, 'Can I give you some feedback?' What happened? Chances are you experienced:

- Increased heart rate
- Heightened blood pressure
- Anxiety and fear
- Defensiveness
- Anger
- Aggression

That's because our brains and bodies have been trained for thousands of years to respond this way. To ensure our existence continued, our ancestors—whether they were jellyfish or cavemen and cavewomen—had to deal with life-threatening events on a regular basis. I am sure the Canadian Neanderthals had to deal with the 'Do I go into this cave or not?' dilemma quite often, knowing that there could be a lurking danger (a bear) waiting to prey on them.

In these situations, there were two decisions—or mistakes—that could be made. One: worry there was a bear in the cave, and therefore not go in. Consequence? Your anxiety prevents you from entering into the warm cave so you freeze your butt off until you find somewhere else to sleep. Or two: you decide the coast is clear, waltz into the cave only to be mauled. Consequence? Great pain or death.

These two decisions have two very different consequences. Anxiety or the end. "This is why we are super-sensitive to apparent threats," explains psychologist Rick Hanson. "Your brain is continually looking for bad news. As soon as it finds some, it fixates on it with tunnel vision, fast-tracks it into memory storage, and then reactivates it at the least hint of anything even vaguely similar. But good news gets a kind of neural shrug: 'uh, whatever.' "

"That's why Mother Nature wants you to make the first mistake (for example, avoid the cave) a thousand times over in order to avoid making the second mistake (getting mauled) even once."[80]

So our bodies are super-sensitive to threats. Our brains perceive feedback as a social threat. When we receive feedback, we are concerned with being ousted from the pack. When we give it, the same occurs.

Then the almighty amygdala comes into play. This is the part of the brain that is on the lookout for threats. A good chunk of the neurons in this part of the brain have been trained for thousands of years to look for the negative. This is where the term 'negativity bias' comes from. Negativity bias suggests we are programmed to focus more on the negative (fear) than the positive (happy).* When we receive feedback, the amygdala kicks up a stink, primes a fight-or-flight response and throws any type of analytical reasoning out the door. Now, in the days of bears and caves, this probably served us well. However, in relation to the 'threats' of the modern workplace, this response is more of a hindrance.

In some ways, it could be so much easier if we had the powers of Nick Marshall, Mel Gibson's character in the movie *What Women Want*, and could hear what others were thinking. Then giving and receiving feedback would be a breeze. It would be timely (instantaneous), truthful (probably a little blunt) and you'd know where you stood. Until we reach that point, we will have to rely on the old-fashioned way ... actually sharing it with each other.

---

* Interestingly, our brains are trained to store negative experiences quickly and for a long time, whereas positive experiences need to be held in awareness for 12 seconds or longer to be stored in our long-term memory.

Where do we start?

When it comes to giving and receiving feedback, there are a number of approaches, which we'll go through a little later on in this chapter. Regardless of which approach is best for your team, there is one thing that is critical at all times. And that is a growth mindset.

Carol Dweck, Professor of Psychology at Stanford University, has devoted a good chunk of her life to examining people's self-conception or mindsets used to guide their behaviour. She often talks about fixed and growth mindsets. Dweck suggests people with a fixed mindset believe their qualities, intelligence and creativity are fixed and cannot change. Whereas those with a growth mindset, believe they can change and see mistakes as a learning opportunity.

Table 21: How we see things differently depending on our mindset

Fixed Mindset	How Teams See	Growth Mindset
Cannot change	Skills & Intelligence	Gained over time
Fluffy, hard to measure. soft	Psychological Safety	Foundation of team development
Appearances	Concerns	Developing
Cannot overcome	Challenges	Possibilities
Embarrasing	Mistakes	What can I learn?
Take it personally; get defensive	Feedback	Appreciative; critical for development
Only use when struggling	Effort	Component of development

Think of mindsets like writing a note to someone. A fixed mindset is similar to how the Flintstones would communicate through writing. If Barney Rubble needed to leave a note for his wife Betty, he'd chisel away at it and his words would be set in stone forever. Barney could only communicate one message and he couldn't change it.

Alternatively, a growth mindset is similar to how we can now write a note. If I need to leave my wife a note, I can start to write one then make changes easily (erase it, cross it out, toss out the piece of paper and start all over again). If I change my thinking, I can either call her or send her a text. I can adapt and choose a different way.

So regardless of how you give or receive feedback, it all starts with your mindset. "For twenty years," writes Dweck, "my research has shown that *the view you adopt for yourself* profoundly affects the way you lead your life."[81]

When it comes to feedback, those with a growth mindset will see feedback as a way to reassess, consider what could be done differently and make positive changes. On the flip side, for those with a fixed mindset, feedback will be seen as a personal attack and the fight-or-flight response will dominate over and over and over.

Feedback doesn't mean you suck anymore

Giving and receiving feedback can suck because old-school ways of giving feedback are often about telling people how they suck. To help you think about productive ways of providing feedback, consider my Five F's of New School Feedback.

Table 22: Old School ways of giving feedback versus New School feedback

Old School	When it comes to ...	New School
Align to my way	Intent	Facilitate understanding
Opinions	Content	Fact based
Past	Focus	Future
One way	Conversation	Flows each way
Episodic	How often	Frequent

Facilitate understanding. These types of discussions need to be about both people seeking to understand. If feedback is used only to get the other person to align with your thinking – don't call it feedback. Call it directing, which is what it actually is.

Fact based. Feedback has to be based on facts. Full stop. If you are providing an opinion, be upfront that it is an opinion, and not a fact. Otherwise be prepared for a different opinion and a potential war of words. Facts cannot be debated; opinions can. Opinions can be dangerous in a feedback situation.

Future focussed. Focus on what needs to happen in the future. Avoid the pit of going on and on about the past. It's done, share the facts, move on and work out what can be done in the future to be better.

Frequent. Whilst episodic feedback is sometimes necessary, incorporating feedback into your discussions regularly means it becomes easier to give and receive, and meaningful progress can be made more quickly.

Flow. To ensure feedback is productive, the conversation has to be just that, a conversation. This means information flows back and forth to ensure both sides are understood.

Tips for effective uses of feedback

1. **Ensure your team members are in the right mindset to hear it**
   Peter Gray, our mate from Boston College, suggests that "it's important to recognize that it's human nature not to want unsolicited negative advice".[82] So before you provide the feedback, ask your team member if they would like you to share some with them or if there is a better time. You could give them a heads up you'd like to chat – let their body process that a (perceived) social threat may be coming. Depending on what you are talking about, it could be something as simple as, 'Can I ask you about something that happened in that meeting?' or 'I've been given some feedback from others about something that happened yesterday that I need to share with you. Is now a good time to share it with you?' Or if it's a little more serious, be straightforward – 'I'd like to talk about x, when's a good time to talk about it?'

   What this does is allow the person to prepare for the 'threat'. As soon as you say this, recognise their fight-or-flight response will kick in, so give them a second to catch their breath.

2. **Pick the right spot**

   This could be a no-brainer, but let's quickly go over it. Find a private, safe spot to have the conversation without others around or able to hear. I've had some of my most difficult discussions over a walk outside. Other times, a meeting room works just fine.

3. **Do it as part of the regular conversation**

   A client of mine once said, "Things are going well when feedback becomes part of the conversation instead of needing to be an event." I really like this. This is the opposite of what Ben and Nate from Gallup discovered. They suggested traditional feedback is still old-school – usually "one direction (manager to employee), episodic (that is, infrequent and isolated) and focused on past mistakes that can't be fixed".[83]

Here are some examples of how to make feedback part of your regular discussions in a team environment:

- *Personalised cards.* Jack Welch, CEO of General Electric, has been criticised for being cutthroat in his business decisions and demand for profitable outcomes. One practice we can learn from Jack is this little gem. Jack provided feedback 'formally' four times a year. Each quarter he would provide his direct reports with a little card, with a handwritten message saying, 'Here's what I like about what you're doing. And here's what you need to improve.'

- *Monthly 1:1 progress reviews with individuals.* Include simple statements, such as 'Here's what I think you could keep doing next month, and here's what you could start doing'. And of course, follow that up with 'What are your thoughts?'

- *Team retros.* Agile methodologies employ 'retrospective reviews' after sprints (chunks of work) with their squads (teams). These help squads improve performance. Employ a similar approach with your team after a meeting, project or a period of time (for example, a month). Ask the team to answer these questions on a piece of paper or sticky note.

  - What did we/you do well?
  - What could we/you have done better?
  - What do we/you need to do well in the next month to make meaningful progress?

  Then have each person share their answers and agree as a group what the next steps are. This approach starts to make feedback part of the discussion and helps lead into 1:1 discussions where feedback can be shared.

Make an event of it asap. If you have feedback about a specific incident, address it asap. It doesn't have to be a 'grand opening' type of event, but a simple, 'Hey, can we talk about something that happened in today's meeting?' type of event. If you wait days or longer, the facts of the feedback can get blurry – for you and them. You'll also feel better if you do it sooner than later. The longer you wait, the more it will take up your mental energy, and if the feedback isn't provided, things will not suddenly get better, the mistake will continue to take place and you'll go batty.

How to get better at giving feedback

The more you and your team share feedback over time, the more natural it will feel for you all. A couple of ways to get more comfortable making feedback part of the conversation include:

- *Ask for it.* The best way to open doors to giving feedback is to first show you are open to receiving it. Take the lead and ask questions such as 'How am I going for you?', 'What could I do that would work better for you?' and 'What do you think I could do differently in the future to be more effective in _____?' You will start to open the door to these discussions, people will start to ask you for feedback and it will soon become part of the regular discussion.
- *Practice.* Find someone senior you trust, ask them for 15 minutes of their time and their feedback on the feedback you'd like to give your team member. By asking someone senior, you can leverage their experience. You'll also be able to receive feedback in return. And it never hurts for people in senior roles to see that you are trying to improve yourself.
- *Tell your teammates.* Mention to them that you're working on your ability to provide feedback and ask them if over the next little while it would be ok if you put extra emphasis on sharing feedback if the opportunity arose. This then opens the door for you to provide feedback, makes you accountable, and will take the edge off for the recipient when you begin the feedback conversation.
- *Provide feedforward.* Someone pretty switched on came up with this term (I don't recall who, sorry!). Rather than focussing on the past, which cannot be changed, focus on what behaviours

would be ideal in the future. 'What would need to happen for you to be able to make it to our meetings on time?' or 'What could you do next time to ensure Jenny feels like she was heard and her opinions were taken on board?' By focussing on the future, you give the person the opportunity to make a productive adjustment and avoid worrying about the past.

Templates for giving feedback

Have you heard of the sandwich model for providing feedback? It's the one where you start off by providing a piece of positive feedback (a piece of bread), then a piece of negative feedback (the meat, or salad, or chicken schnitzel), then another piece of positive feedback (the other piece of bread). The idea and metaphor are great. However, no disrespect, but I think this is a shit sandwich. Remember the idea of negative bias? How many times have you told someone multiple good things about them, and one thing to work on, and what do they hang onto? The one thing to work on. That's because we are trained to focus on the threat to survive. So if you want to reinforce certain behaviours, reinforce away. If there are some behaviours that need to be changed, have a specific conversation about those behaviours, and those behaviours only.

Simple, right? If not, here are three ways to help make these types of conversations easier.

When you ... I feel ...
This is good for when a particular behaviour has an impact on you. It sounds like, 'When you did x, I felt y. What do you think?' For this to work, there are three important things to keep in mind:

1. **Focus on the behaviour and ensure the feedback is factual.** What was the specific action the person took? 'When you showed up to the meeting late for the third time this week ...' instead of, 'You always show up late'. Or, 'When you called my idea outdated ...' instead of 'You made me look stupid'. Can you see the difference? If you keep the 'when you' focussed on facts, you are well set up to gain a shared understanding of what happened. If you don't, you then get into a debate over what actually happened. Which is another shit sandwich to deal with.

2. **Share how you feel, not that you feel that.** Listen to yourself. If you share how you feel—sad, happy, scared, intimidated, worthless—there is no debate. It's how you actually feel. If you say 'I feel that ...' – it automatically becomes an opinion.

3. **Invite a conversation.** This is where Nate and Ben's ideas (from Gallup) around coaching conversations come into play. The key word being *conversation*. When you finish up with your 'I feel', cap it off with a 'What do you think?' These four words can turn an 'event' into a conversation.

Note: Some would also add in a 'because' ('When you ... I felt ... because ... What do you think?'). If you do, once again, the 'because' has to be factual. Opinions will open up a can of worms, because it is your opinion, and let's be honest, who says your opinion is the right one?

When the stakes are high
Georgia Murch, author of *Fixing Feedback* (a great read, by the way), suggests when providing really important feedback, it's critical to ensure it is given *and* the relationship preserved. She also says people hear your content and smell your intent. So ensure your

feedback intent is authentic – otherwise you'll be found out very soon. Love it, Georgia!

This is where a curiosity mindset makes a difference. When you go in with a curiosity mindset, the discussion becomes a flow of information, exchanged by two curious adults ... and people feel safe because they smell your intent.

So to kickstart the conversation—and that's what you need to do—start the conversation. Here are seven steps you can take to kick off the conversation, share your feedback and hear what your colleagues think ... in less than 90 seconds.* Yes, 90 seconds. Remember – feedback is about facilitating understanding and is a flow of information back and forth.

1. **State the issue**

   Get right to the point. 'Alex, I need to talk about how we are working together.' Avoid talking about the weather, the last meeting, what's on for the weekend. Rip the band-aid off, state the issues as clearly and succinctly as you can. See if you can do it in 10 words or less.

2. **Provide examples**

   Start with facts. If your examples are factual, you are giving your colleague the opportunity to develop an understanding of where you are coming from. This allows the conversation to stay on track about the issue. If you start with your opinions—or your interpretation of the situation—the conversation will go off track and get lost in whose opinion is right or wrong. Your opinion matters, just not right now.

---

* I can't take credit for developing this approach, but think it works wonders. I've seen various versions of it, the first one from the IECL during my training as an executive coach.

Keep your examples short and sweet (and have more information about each fact if need be down the track). Provide up to three examples. If there are any more, the conversation can turn into a lecture (or as Georgia says, a "yoursation"). Remember, this is about starting a conversation to create shared understanding. It's not a lecture.

3. **Share your feelings or emotions about the issues**

   Once you've established facts about why you have an issue to discuss, you can now share your feelings. You're human, you have emotions. Be open, vulnerable and share how your colleague's behaviours have made YOU feel. Avoid 'I feel that ...' which often leads to an opinion, which can be contested.

4. **Clarify what's at stake**

   You need to be very clear at this point. You can clarify what's at stake for you, and what's at stake for them. 'This is important because what's at stake is ...' is a good starter. For many, this part is a challenge because there are often negative consequences if the issue is not remedied. However, with a mindset of creating shared understanding, it's important both of you understand what's at stake.

5. **Identify your contribution**

   If you've got a mirror, this is the time to look into it. If you have contributed to the issue in any way, be honest and share how you've contributed. If you haven't, then you can skip this step. But if you've changed your mind back and forth and created a level of confusion, if you've avoided having this conversation or you've forged forward without getting your colleague's inputs – whatever it might be, put it forward right now and own it. This approach demonstrates shared accountability.

   A word of advice. Be totally honest with yourself. When you say 'I may have', 'I might have', 'I can see how you could have interpreted this to mean x when I meant y' ... you aren't owning it. 'I was not clear', 'I didn't check in with you' or 'This happened in the past and I avoided bringing it up' – that's owning it.

6. **Identify your desire to resolve the issue**

    You've come this far – now is the time to state what you'd like. 'I really want to resolve this.'

    That's it. State your desire. And start to gain an understanding from their perspective

7. **Ask for their thoughts**

    I love internationally recognised business advisor and author Ron Price's quote about conversations. He says, "There are two experts in every conversation: I am the expert of my intent and you are the expert of my impact."

    You have your intent and you've stated it. Now comes the chance to understand the impact of your intent (the conversation starter). Something as simple as: 'What do you think?' 'What are your thoughts?'

And that's it. Well done, you've started the conversation.

Table 20: Overview of feedback conversation starters

I'd like to talk to you about ...
What I've observed is ...
Those observations make me feel/assume/believe ...
It's important to resolve this because what's at stake is ...
I haven't made it better – I ...
And what I'd like is to make it better.
What are your thoughts?

Practice makes perfect

Tatchakorn Yeerum, a Buddhist monk (better known as Tony Jaa, the martial artist, actor and stuntman), said he practices martial arts "not to win over other people, but to win over my own heart". When it comes to feedback conversations, it's important to practice too. Not just for your colleagues, but for yourself. I'm a big believer in writing things down to clarify my thoughts. I often practice using the seven-step process which involves writing down my thoughts and by the end of the last step, I've realised two things:

1. What I thought was the issue wasn't the real issue
2. I feel much better about my approach and what I want to get out of the conversation

So win your own heart and practice. Here are five tips to help you practice:

1. Write down the seven steps and add bullet points below each step. Fill in the blanks. Heck, you can even bring your notes into your discussion. Nothing says 'I care about this conversation' like showing you've prepared for it.
2. Say your feedback out loud to yourself.
3. Time yourself. If it's slightly over a minute, you're ok. If it starts to get longer than 90 seconds, revisit your content and get to the point more quickly.
4. Find a trusted colleague and ask them, 'How does this sound?' I did this once with a former manager and he very perceptively pointed out I was making a number of assumptions. Practicing

with a colleague saved me from looking like a complete ass and helped set the tone for an interesting conversation.

5. Record yourself. Either with video or sound alone. You'll be amazed at what you see and what you hear. If you're like me, you may realise how serious you look and develop cues to remind yourself to be more empathetic.

Remember – we are talking about a one-minute conversation starter. Book a room for 20 minutes, practice, make a change or two, practice a couple of times and you are well on your way to gaining some meaningful insights.

Receiving feedback

Receiving feedback is like getting a needle at the doctor. It stings but does help you down the track. And if done properly, it only stings for a second.

I read somewhere about receiving feedback that you need to be prepared to admit that it just might be accurate. And when you give it, you may want to be ready to duck. Even though I'm a baseball fan, I'd suggest more admission than throwing. Outside of getting defensive and discounting the feedback, there are steps you can take to ensure you work on your admission skills instead of your throwing ones. They include:

- *Take a breath.* Remember, your brain hears feedback, thinks bears, and reacts accordingly. Take a breath to calm yourself, lower your heart rate and manage the adrenaline that will be entering your system.

- There is a Saskatoon proverb that says, '*Examine what is said, not him or her who is saying it.*'* Focus on the content and on choosing a mindset of understanding and growth. There is a learning opportunity in every discussion we have. Choose to learn.
- Consider a second Saskatoon proverb. '*Examine who is saying it, not just what is being said.*'** The person giving you feedback is human. Chances are they are uncomfortable giving it and concerned about the impact of how it will be received. Choose an appreciative mindset when hearing feedback.
- *Acknowledge what you've heard.* Focus on clarifying what needs to happen in the future. Fight the fight-or-flight instinct. A simple question such as 'What would make it better down the track?' is a good way to move forward productively. If you aren't sure what would make things better – say that. And ask for your colleague's help or their opinion.
- *Thank them.* With a growth mindset, you can benefit from the feedback. As my parents taught my two brothers and I, make sure you say thanks when someone does something nice for you.

There is one other way to make receiving feedback even easier ... and that's asking for it.

---

* To be honest, I am pretty sure it isn't a Saskatoon proverb. However, in my research, one source says it's an African proverb. Another says Arabian. And yet another says Egyptian. So I am going to stir the pot a bit and throw Saskatoon into the mix, with the disclosure I am not 100% sure where the proverb originated.

** I came up with this one and am going to attribute it as a Saskatoon proverb.

Getting the feedback you want by asking for it

One way to avoid those initial awkward physiological and emotional responses when someone asks you if you'd like some feedback is to get on the front foot and ask for it yourself. When individuals demonstrate this level of desire and vulnerability, it can only make it easier for others to align.

Have you ever completed a 360-degree review process through an automated online system? A number of peers and colleagues rate you on key skills and capabilities. You receive a report with the average of the scores on those skills and capabilities, as well as a number of bullet point responses to open-ended questions where you spend half your time trying to work out who said what, and what might have driven their responses at the time. Sound familiar? These types of systems make it easy to collect a large number of people's responses together in an efficient time frame (assuming you don't have to chase up everyone to complete their responses). The reports also help provide some direction for further discussion with your colleagues, leader or HR. Or to keep on file for updating your resume under the 'strengths' area.

To get meaningful feedback and contribute to an environment where feedback conversations become the norm for teams, simply asking and listening can be just as—if not more—effective than a formal 360-degree process. You will gain context and clarity, and create a much safer environment for those you are asking. You also save valuable mental energy not trying to work out who said what!

Detractors of this approach will challenge whether or not you will get honest feedback. It's a fair comment, particularly when you are dealing with people who report to you. Often reports hold back because they feel their feedback may impact their image or security. However, if asked correctly, you'll find yourself not only getting valuable insights, but you'll be setting up your team environment so it's one where these kinds of discussions can become the norm.

Case Study: Leaders asking for feedback in a group setting

One of the first times I encountered this approach was at Novartis Pharmaceuticals. This was the same team I mentioned earlier that was a shining team. We were at a two-day planning offsite with four teams from Saskatchewan and Manitoba. We were in a meeting room, tables set up in a U shape, computer in the middle of the table on the bottom of the U. Our manager Liz asked one of the team members to be the typist and for all of us to answer three questions: 'What can I do better, more of and less of' in relation to how she supported us as a manager. She said she was going to leave the room for half an hour and asked us to answer the questions honestly. For the next half-hour, we spoke as a team about what Liz did that worked and what didn't. When Liz came in, she read through out loud what we had typed, asked for some clarification on a couple of points and then thanked us for our feedback. Her body language and facial expression didn't change – she was smiling the whole time.

Years later when I asked her about this approach, her biggest piece of advice was, "Make it spontaneous. You'll have their initial thoughts and reactions which I believe are much more authentic, useful and actionable."

You may be at a stage where you can ask these questions yourself and stay in the room. Here are the keys to asking and receiving meaningful feedback in a group or 1:1 setting:

- Keep the questions simple and specific. Think of the power of three – ask no more than three questions to kick off the conversation excluding clarifying questions.
- Once team members start responding, smile, nod, listen and take notes. Avoid justifying. Smile, nod, listen and take notes.
- To gain greater insights to a response, simple follow-ups like 'Can you tell me more about that?', 'What impact does that have on you?' or 'What would be a better way to manage that?'
- Smile, nod, listen and take notes.
- (This should be starting to sound familiar – remember ALE: ask, listen and explore?)
- At the end – thank the team. It may not have been easy for you to ask, and it most likely wasn't easy for them to respond. Recognise this and show your appreciation.

Questions to ask to get meaningful feedback
Keeping in the spirit of threes, here are four sets of three questions you could use to start your own feedback discussion. If participants suggest 'I need some time to think about this' … I'd respond with 'That would be great. But just off the top of your head, what would you say?' Either way you'll get some actionable insights and demonstrate you value feedback conversations.

Questions to ask your leader
- When I am at my best, what am I doing?
- When I am not at my best, what am I doing?

- Specifically, what do I need to work on to be ready for [insert the job or assignment you're most interested in here]?
- If your boss (as in, your leader's boss) was to give me one piece of advice, what would it be?
- Who could I be working more closely with?
- Which parts of my style concern you the most?

Questions to ask your team
- What could I do more of that would help you be at your best?
- What could I do less of to help you be at your best?
- Where am I taking up the most of your time?
- Tell me what you're getting from me that you find valuable.
- Tell me what I'm doing that gets in the way.
- What specifically can I do to better support our team's mission?

And for every single question – be sure to follow it up with 'What else?' You could legitimately ask this question three times, and if you are comfortable with a little silence in between responses, you'll unearth some useful insights.

Who could I ask?

Let's move beyond asking for feedback from the obvious – your boss, your teammates and those who report into you. What about your boss's boss? A supplier? A customer? Someone who you work with on a project? A mentor? Think about who you spend a decent amount of time with at work. In one organisation I sat across from the Director of Corporate Affairs. We did little work directly together but during an informal discussion, he shared with me his perspective on how I handled difficult discussions based on what he heard when I was on the phone (thanks Roger!).

Liz, my manager at Novartis, scared the living daylights out of me once when, during a face-to-face call with a doctor, she asked the doctor for some feedback on what he thought I did well and what I could do better. I nearly shat my dacks, worried about what he would say. However, the feedback he gave me was extremely useful and I remembered it every time I walked into a GP's clinic. I've since used this approach with some of my team members and it's been a useful exercise for everyone involved.

Here's another for you. What about asking your partner, parents or siblings? You'll be amazed by what you will discover by asking them 'What do you think I do well?' or 'What do you think I am not good at?' See what parallels you can draw from their responses to how you work with your team.

Let's not forget the obvious – positive feedback that doesn't suck

Have you ever been walking around your house, or the office, looking for your phone, when you realised you were talking on it? Ok, maybe it's just me then, but at times, things are so obvious we sometimes miss them.

Giving positive feedback is an obvious action we could be doing but we sometimes overlook. OfficeVibe's feedback report showed that 69% of employees say they would work harder if they felt their efforts were better recognised. However, the negative bias can often override the positive bias and too many times we tend to focus on 'what could be better' instead of acknowledging what's going well.

Getting and giving positive feedback is like eating ice cream on a hot day – it feels great. It also reinforces what needs to be done, it recognises you've done something good and it's a great form of gratitude. Giving positive feedback can seem straightforward but here are four tips to ensure it makes the biggest impact possible.

1. **Recognise effort over natural ability**. Carol Dweck (the godmother of the growth mindset concept) conducted a study with children, identifying what types of positive feedback have the greatest impact on learning behaviours. When assigned task #1, a group was praised for their efforts ('You must have worked really hard') and another for a natural ability ('You must be smart at this'). When given a second task, each participant was given the choice between a harder task or easier task. Of those who were originally praised for their *efforts*, 90% chose the harder tasks; the majority of those who were praised for their *intelligence* chose the easier task. And when a third task was assigned—one as easy as task #1—the group who were praised for *effort* improved their scores by 30%. The group who were praised for their *intelligence*? Their score declined by 20%. "When we praise children for their intelligence," Dweck wrote, "we tell them that's the name of the game: look smart, don't risk making mistakes."[84]

   This type of feedback also sounds like a good way to create a psychologically safe environment.

2. **Be specific about the inputs**. 'You presented really well!', 'You are a great communicator', 'You are really good with customers.' These sound great, don't they. But which behaviours do they actually reinforce? Focus on the inputs – what specifically did the

person do in the presentation? What do they do that makes them a great communicator? Do they listen more than they speak? Do they prepare well? The more specific you can be the better.

3. **Have fun with it**. You can share your feedback face-to-face. Or on a postcard. A sticky note. A text. A video. Have someone else share the feedback. Imagine getting a note from your CEO telling you he was impressed with the selection of the story you shared during a presentation to the finance team ... and he wasn't even there, but heard about it from a colleague.

4. **Be deliberate about providing positive feedback**. What you focus on is what you'll see. At one of my workshops, a participant shared that "Each week, I would choose one person to focus on, look for something good and send them a postcard that week with the feedback." Love this.

My mate Joe Maddon shared his view on feedback: "If I am honest with you now, you may not like me for a couple of days. If I lie to you, you will hate me forever."

This was one of the reasons Joe was so well-respected amongst his players. He once shared a story about providing feedback to a player who struggled to stick in the big leagues. Joe's feedback related to how the player's work effort was perceived, which was not good. The player had no idea this was the perception. As a result, the player made some changes and was able to improve how he was perceived. Had Joe not provided the feedback, this player could have continued to ride the merry-go-round, going from club to club, without knowing what the problem was.

Key Takeaways

☑ When it comes to receiving, asking for or giving feedback, remember it all starts with your mindset. Choose a fixed mindset and as philosopher Elbert Hubbard once said, "To avoid criticism, do nothing, say nothing, and be nothing." Choose a growth mindset and you will learn and evolve.

☑ When engaging in a feedback conversation, remember the Five F's of Feedback: Facilitate understanding, make it Fact based, ensure information Flows each way, focus on the Future, and do it Frequently.

☑ Remember the power of positive reinforcement. Look for specific moments of brilliance and praise the inputs over the outputs.

Reflections

💡 Who has given you the most useful feedback and what impact did it have on you?

💡 When was the last time you asked each person on your team for feedback? Do you think that's enough?

💡 Who do I need to initiate a feedback conversation with?

CHAPTER 17

Creating relationships with conflict

When there is no fighting, that's when there are problems.
~ Ben Darwin, ex-Australian Wallaby and co-founder of
GainLine Analytics

When it comes to Canada and sports, people automatically think of (ice) hockey.* Probably curling and maybe even ski jumping. Not traditionally known as a basketball country, the sport's popularity increased significantly when the Vancouver Grizzlies and Toronto Raptors joined the NBA in 1995. Even more so when in 2018, the Raptors became the first non-American team to win the Larry O'Brien Championship Trophy. (I didn't know this until I wrote this book, but the Larry O'Brien Trophy is awarded to the team who wins the NBA playoffs.) The Raptors had flirted with the notion of becoming NBA champs in the past, but it took a gutsy firing, a controversial trade and a different approach from their new head coach to get them over

---

* As someone who grew up with a pair of skates on from when I was five years old and spent a good chunk of my childhood playing (ice) hockey, it pains me somewhat to have to refer to the sport as *ice* hockey. To my ice hockey fans reading this, yes in fact there is another hockey, field hockey. And true fact – in field hockey you are NOT allowed to shoot left-handed. The sticks and rules are designed to prevent this from happening. Odd ... but odd can be good, as can conflict.

the line. Head Coach Dwayne Casey was fired in May 2018.* Assistant Coach Nick Nurse was promoted to the top job and not long after the new coaching appointment, GM Masai Ujiri traded fan favourite DeMar DeRozan for superstar Kawhi Leonard.

Nick Nurse was no stranger to coaching. He got his first college coaching gig at the age of 23, coached for 11 years in Europe before returning to the US to coach in the NBA's Development League. In 2013 he made his entrance into the NBA coaching ranks with the Raptors as an assistant.

One of Nurse's guiding principles is when there is an elephant in the room, address it before it cripples the team. Whether it's a difference of opinions, a bad game or tiff amongst the players or the coaches, his goal is to talk about it sooner than later. As Josh Lewenberg from TSN reported, "Nurse has a small elephant figurine in his office to symbolize how he wants his team to deal with conflict: head on."

Conflict often has negative connotations. And in some ways rightfully so. Conflict often arises when people feel threatened. Someone ate my chocolate in the fridge. Someone has a different idea than me, thinks I am wrong, or worse yet, proved that I was wrong. Or someone apparently called me an idiot behind my back. Boom! Our fight-or-flight reaction is activated. In 2008, CPP Global conducted a survey on workplace conflict across nine countries and 5,000 employees. They reported the majority of employees at all levels experience conflict to some degree, and found that in the US, employees spend 2.8 hours per week dealing with unproductive conflict,** equating to approximately US$359 billion in paid hours.

** Professional coaching is a tough gig. Casey was fired from the Raptors only to be named the NBA's Coach of the Year five weeks after his dismissal.

*** Folks working in Ireland and Germany apparently spent the most time in conflict – roughly 3.3 hours per week. Australia and Canada were not part of the survey. If you search for *Workplace conflict and how businesses can harness it to thrive*, you'll find the whole report.

Whoa ... that's massive bucks. You'd sure hope there is a strong ROI on that investment.

Good, bad or ugly?

Ok, so unproductive conflict costs big bucks. It impacts quality of work, engagement, retention (resignations and firings), stress and absenteeism. The list goes on.

However, there is a broader spectrum to consider when it comes to conflict. I quoted Ben Darwin at the beginning of this chapter as he and I often debate whether you need to like the people on your team to be high performing. Ben and his business partner Simon Strachan help organisations set up teams and structures based on their Cohesion Analytics. Ben also represented the Australian National Rugby Union team in the early 2000s so brings some great sporting and corporate insights into the high performance area. We've run Leadership Performance Labs and his view is you don't have to like each other to perform well. I agree—there are many examples—but I also say, imagine what would happen if you did like each other, how much better performance could be. One thing we do agree on is that disagreement and conflict are instrumental in higher performance.

Take the approach of the Wright brothers. They would often 'debate'. Debate = heated arguments. They were brothers and as brothers do, they had more than the odd debate ... but look at where they ended up. Inventors of the airplane! At times, midway through their 'debates' they would switch sides and start to argue the other's point of view. By the end of the argument, Orville would be arguing for Wilbur's point and vice versa. Or they would throw out both ideas and identify a better third option. Whether they knew it or not, they were using the 'Dissoi Logoi' approach. In Greek, the words mean 'double arguments' and represent the concept of opposing arguments, a cornerstone of Sophistic ideology and method.

How to use conflict in a good way

When using conflict in this manner, Orville and Wilbur had chosen to enter into the Inner Sanctum of Conflict. I created the Sanctums of Conflict to help demonstrate how conflict can work for or against teams. It's been really useful when working with leaders and teams to help remind them how to initiate, respond to or manage conflict in a productive way.

Table 24: The Sanctums of Conflict

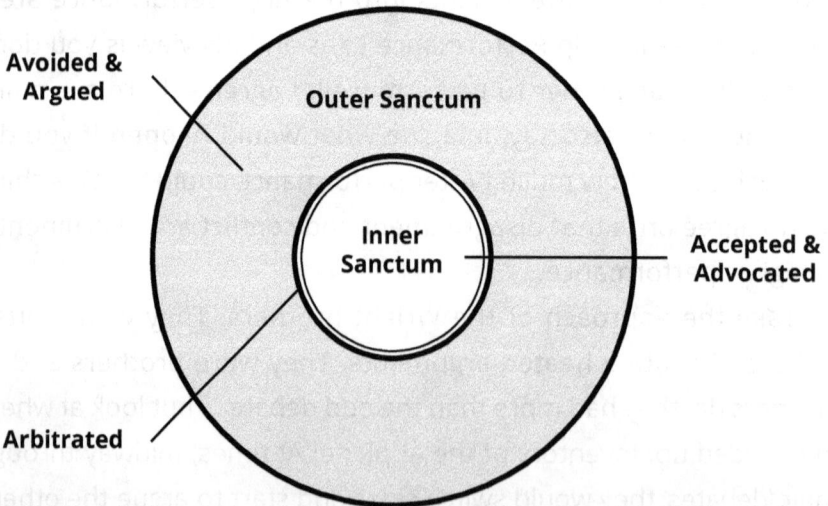

The *Inner Sanctum of Conflict* is a place where conflict is used productively. It is characterised by:

- Focussing on the 'what' – seeking to understand the challenge, the solution, the issue
- Effectiveness
- Listening things through and talking things through
- Humility and emotional sensitivity
- Persuasion and persuaded

The *Outer Sanctum of Conflict* is where conflict causes people and teams pain. It is characterised by:

- Focussing on the who
- Inefficiencies
- Arrogance, aggressiveness and rudeness
- Emotional responses
- Manipulation and bulldozing

You'll notice there is a small area in between the two sanctums which is sometimes required when a solution cannot be achieved but is necessary. Think of this as going to Mommy and Daddy to sort out your issues.

In the 2008 CPP Human Capital Report, the top three benefits of conflict identified were:

- Better understanding of others
- Improved working relationships
- Better solutions to a problem

I believe teams that embrace conflict—and actually advocate for it—will be much more effective, perhaps up to 20 times more effective than those who avoid it.

Table 25: Impact of managing conflict effectively

Roles leaders can play	Impact
Advocator	20x
Approver	10x
Arbitrator	5x
Arguer	2x
Avoider	1x

How to enter the Inner Sanctum

Conflict often arises because of someone's desire to be right. The term 'confirmation bias' supports this. Confirmation bias is our tendency to interpret new evidence as confirmation of our existing beliefs. Research has shown that people have a tendency to seek information that confirms their existing beliefs; this is one of the key barriers to managing conflict productively. Despite our understanding of confirmation bias, we still over-index on the need to be right. When people realise there may be another way to do things, that they can be wrong *and* still make progress, then conflict can work for us instead of against us.

Intellectual humility – the key to the Inner Sanctum of Conflict

Mark Leary is a social and personality psychologist at Duke University. He has studied how to work together while thinking differently. This newly emerging area of psychology is something he calls 'intellectual humility'. According to Mark, intellectual humility (IH) is "the recognition the things you believe might in fact be wrong". Individuals who demonstrate higher scores on intellectual humility tests demonstrate greater openness to hearing opposing views, regularly seek out information that conflicts with their view, pay more attention to evidence, and have a stronger self-awareness when they get something wrong.

Author and researcher Shane Snow references IH in his book *Dream Teams*.* He shares the story of a black gentleman named Malcolm, whose house was burnt down twice by white supremacists, and whose father was killed by a white racist. Eventually, Malcolm became a preacher, advocating that all white people were evil. He started working with the Nazi American Party, to advocate for what both wanted – for blacks and whites to live separately. He and Dr Martin Luther King were at opposite ends of the spectrum – one for integration, the other soundly opposed. Eventually, Malcolm changed his mind. Through a number of experiences, he was able to realise his way was not the right way. As a result, Malcolm—better known as Malcolm X—was able to inspire generations to do better with others.

---

* Shane has also developed an IH test. Here is the link: https://www.shanesnow.com/take-the-intellectual-humility-assessment.

How to put intellectual humility into action

Malcolm X's ability to use IH is a powerful example of how being open to different perspectives can bring about great change. He was able to change his perspective, admit he was wrong and work within the Inner Sanctum of Conflict.

Here are some tips for staying in the Inner Sanctum of Conflict and adopting intellectual humility to make conflict work for you instead of against you.

1. **Swear in front of each other, not behind each other.** Arianna Huffington shared her view on conflict in an interview with *The Four-Hour Work Week* author Tim Ferriss.[85] When there is a strong level of trust between two people, she recommends for them to say things as they are, not to hold back, not to wait to find the exact right words. She said, "You can say it while you are angry. You don't have to wait to calm down. Whatever. But if you're incapable of doing that, if you're only capable of passive-aggressive behavior, which is always being nice to your managers or your colleagues while badmouthing them behind their backs, consider this your last warning. If we say that as clearly as we have said it, and not just I but everybody here, but you can't do it, then this is not the right place for you." Perhaps Aussie tennis player Bernard Tomic could have taken this on board in early 2019. There was some obvious conflict within the Australian Davis Cup team. In front of the media, Bernard Tomic blasted his captain Lleyton Hewitt. Tomic suggested to reporters that no one (including teammates Nick Kyrgios and Thanasi Kokkinakis) liked Hewitt, that Hewitt ruined the system, and questioned publicly why Hewitt was still playing. "You are retired I thought," said Tomic.

Unsurprisingly, the team was ousted (by Canada I might add) in the quarterfinals. Two months later, Nick Kyrgios and Lleyton sat down to clear the air, and at the 2020 Australian Open, it was obvious they were in a better place. Kyrgios went from being ranked #51 to #26 from 2019 to 2020 and Australia qualified for the final four of the 2020 ATP Cup. Experts have suggested they would not have made it that far if Lleyton and Nick had not worked on their relationship. Bernard Tomic? At one stage of his career he was ranked as high as 17th in the world. In January 2020 – he was ranked 183rd.

For those of us who the media doesn't really care about, it's easy for us to talk or swear about someone behind their back. The reality is it's gutless and childish. Instead, save your energy, have a discussion, share your perspective and see where the conversation can lead you.

2. **Pick your battles.** We've all known people like this. Heck, we may even have been one of them. You know, the one who has an answer to everything. Rather than be a know-it-all, choose your battles wisely to ensure when you voice your opinion, eyes open up instead of roll back. Keep in mind intellectual humility isn't about rolling over and giving in all the time. You are smart, you've got a seat at the table for a reason. Be sure to stand strong ... sometimes.

3. **Be emotional about an outcome.** Liane Davey, author of *The Good Fight*, wrote that "conflict in the workplace is never about facts. If it was about facts, we'd be problem-solving. It (conflict) is about our emotions." This is why IH is so important. Those with IH can reframe their role in the discussion as working towards a solution and not about their idea being chosen. When it becomes about *your* idea, it becomes about you, which is the

wrong thing to get emotional about. Choose a mindset that says hey, it's super important we can get an outcome we can all live with. And then get emotional with that outcome in mind.

4. **Use open-ended questions.** 'What if', 'What might happen', 'What could', 'If we were to consider this option, what would be a positive outcome?', 'How can we do both?' When you use language like this, possibilities open up. By avoiding definitive statements ('The right way to …' or 'The best way to …'), you demonstrate you are open-minded and can think about things differently.

5. **Focus on the future.** Avoid the blame game. When the blame game starts, it's game over. The defense mechanisms kick in and the conversation will turn into an argument. By focussing on the future, it shows you are ready to move on and find a solution.

How to get your team better at using conflict productively

To help your team become more comfortable with conflict, think of the 5C's of Conflict and how they can help your team work together. The 5C's of Conflict are: Commit, Challenge, Compete, Conceal and Champion.

Commit to wrong being a possibility. Prior to a meeting, commit to the idea that each person in the room could be wrong. By asking for that promise, it sets the tone for a discussion where it's ok to be wrong or not have all the answers.

Challenge on purpose. Ask someone to purposefully be the challenger at a team meeting. Get them to challenge at least two ideas. Use the 'Dissoi Logoi' approach like the Wright brothers. Or use a Red Team approach. When you can't agree on a direction, pick a solution and purposefully assign someone to work out how that plan could potentially fail. The key to this activity is to ensure that people know the aim of the activity is to be purposefully critical of the idea, not the person whose solution you chose.

Compete. Have you ever asked your kids to do something and said, 'I'll time you to see how long it takes' to get their mind off the task and onto action? Competition can channel some amazing activity and outcomes. In Chapter 2, I mentioned the Wu-Tang Clan and how Shane Snow considers them a high performing team. In *Dream Teams*, Snow shares his insights into how the Wu-Tang Clan became one of the most successful rap bands of all time by competing with each other when choosing what to record. Founder Robert Diggs, better known as RZA, would give his rappers the beats to a song and they'd have to come back with the lyrics. They would go toe to toe with each other, with Diggs then choosing which lyrics would be recorded. In this case, Diggs was dealing with several A-type personalities, including those from rival gangs. Whilst this type of competition was not always productive (there were some strong disagreements vocalised in less-than-productive ways), it does provide a good lesson. If you decide to take this approach, ensure the group is mature enough to handle a 'defeat'. Or be prepared for some swearing at each other (as long as it's to each other's faces, which is much more productive than swearing behind each other's backs!). If you can also throw some fun into your competitions (what kind of silly prizes can you come up with for all participants?), even better.

Conceal ideas. When working on a problem with a group of people, ask them to submit their ideas on a piece of paper with no name on it. This will take out some personal bias that may exist. This is particularly effective when you have a room full of senior and junior folks involved. The junior staff rightly or wrongly can feel intimidated; this approach takes away any potential self-doubt issues.

Champion it. I've heard of advertising agencies inviting junior staff into the boardroom and presenting their big-pitch ideas to them as a group. The goal is for the junior staff to identify gaps and assumptions. Finding faults with your superiors' work sounds intimidating, but having leaders champion conflict and different perspectives on their own work encourages all team members to feel more comfortable sharing their opinions in other settings, as well as taking on conflicting views of their own work.

Leaders managing Outer Sanctum behaviours

How many times has a member of your team come to you with a conflict between themselves and another person in the team, looking to you to sort the issue? It used to happen to me a lot. Early on in my career, I felt honoured when this happened. 'You've come to me to help you, that's what I love doing, let me tell you what to do ...' Let's just say when I took on this approach, not only did I end up telling my team how to suck eggs or potentially give them bad advice, it also added to my workload and list of things to worry about. Now that's not to say you should ignore your people, however there are better ways to support your team when it comes to managing their conflict.

Mark Horstman, co-founder of the *Manager Tools* podcast, suggests there are four actions managers tend to take when conflict amongst the team is brought to their attention. Note that most of this approach is Mark's thinking, not mine. I thought it was so good I had to share it.

Table 26: What managers tend to do when conflict is brought to their attention

	Focus On Conflict	
	• Avoid it • Get directive	
Push It		**Make It Personal**
• "I've had enough" • "I don't want to hear about it"		• Focus on the people or the task
	Don't See It	
	• Hear about it after someone resigns	

Rather than take one of these four actions, Mark suggests there are two options a manager can choose when news of conflict comes to their attention.

Option 1: Act
Option 2: Not act

Sometimes things aren't worth acting on. If it's a minor issue, or someone simply needs someone to listen, then this approach can work. You can usually sort out which action to take by asking the other person what you can do to help.

For those who choose to act, Mark points to four key steps to help frame the view of the conflict.

1. **Reinforce your belief in your people.** If you are working with good people, then it's important to remind them that you believe in them, even if their behaviour is not ideal in the case of the conflict. Mark says something as simple as 'You're fine, I value what you do and your behaviour, in this case, is not effective.' This is not the same as the Shit Sandwich Feedback model. It's simply a matter of reminding your team member they are valued even though their behaviour in the current case is not. It's important to remind them they are not under attack from you in terms of the feedback you've given. Conflict in the Outer Sanctum is emotional, so it's important to calm the emotions.

2. **Provide feedback about the conflict management.** The feedback in this case needs to be about the behaviours in relation to the conflict. Not about what could be done to fix the problem. It needs to be focussed on what Outer Sanctum behaviours exist in this situation. Ignore the urge to talk about the actual work conflict. Leave that to your people to sort out. In most cases, your support would be best served in coaching the behaviours associated with managing the conflict.

3. **Encourage an apology.** Mark talks about one of the ways he gauges senior leadership potential in employees, which is their ability to recognise their part in conflict and "be the first one to put out their hand" and apologise. It helps defuse the situation, calms things down and demonstrates that at the moment of apology, they are putting the relationships above solving the problem. Most times, he says, if the conflict is serious enough,

good team members will actually offer an apology as one of the steps. If not, subtly—or not so subtly—you could ask them to.*

4. **Keep the work moving forward.** By having a coaching conversation, you are putting the onus back on the person responsible for sorting the conflict. That means you don't have to be running around putting out fires all day and leaving your to-do list on the backburner. It also gives you permission to follow up at your next 1:1. Ask them – did you apologise? How did you resolve the issue? What do you think contributed to the outcome? Boom! Great questions to reinforce a learning episode for your team members.

In his podcast, Mark outlines how this can all sound so eloquent. It goes something like this: "You're fine, I really value what you bring to this team *and* in this case, your behaviour was ineffective. What could you do to help the issue move forward effectively? Great, I'd love for you to apologise for your actions to them and let me know how the conversation goes."

There is one thing Mark highly recommends avoiding as much as you can. And that's to call the two people involved into your office and talk it out amongst the three of you. This is the arbitration zone. This is the exact approach I take as a parent when my kids are fighting about something. I listen (sort of, mostly I am annoyed I have to sort the issue out). I then tell them what to do. Which works great, right? Until the conflict rears its ugly head up again and again

---

* One of Mark's other pearls of wisdom is to avoid the word 'should'. I try to avoid the word 'hate' (it's such a strong word and there's enough of it in our world). 'But' and 'busy' also drive me nuts. I think 'should' is going on my list now. It's judgemental and could be seen as disrespecting others' abilities to make their own decisions. Mark has actually challenged my thinking and I've since gone through the draft of this book and the word 'should' only appears 15 times (three in this footnote alone).

and I say, 'Why does this keep coming up? I thought we sorted this out.' The answer: because I've directed instead of coached.

The added complexity in an office setting is that typically when two people get called into the principal's office ... er, the boss's office, people can see what's happening. Drama can build up outside the office. The two in your office can see that others can see, and like my boys, will most often do whatever it takes to end the awkward conversation in front of everyone.

Ideally, the two can sort it out themselves. If not, find somewhere away from everyone (nothing like a good walk outside together), look to facilitate the discussion and only if need be, arbitrate and make a decision for them.

If teams aren't managing conflict well, bad things happen. Patrick Lencioni has written about the lead up to the Royal Commission into Misconduct in the Banking, Superannuation and Financial Services Industry:

> Someone knew that someone was charging (insurance premiums to) people who were dead, and instead of standing up in that meeting and saying 'Wait, this is not right' they said 'Oh, I don't want to accuse them, this could be difficult.' You see where the lack of conflict allows people to watch bad things happening and not do something about it.

When it really matters, there is far too much to be gained and far too much to lose by not sharing your opinion. Ask those at NASA, VW or Victoria Police. Ask those at the banks who have had to put in an enormous amount of work to rectify the lack of healthy conflict. Or those who lost their jobs. If you've got a different opinion, say it. Say it sooner. The more you can do it through the Inner Sanctum of Conflict, the more meaningful progress you and your team can make.

Key Takeaways

☑ Using conflict through the Inner Sanctum means conflict is accepted and advocated for. It can make teams 20 times more effective than those who ignore it.

☑ The recognition that what you believe might be wrong—known as intellectual humility—is critical to making progress when conflict arises.

☑ Apologising for your behaviours while in conflict demonstrates you value the relationship over the outcomes.

Reflections

🔆 When was the last time you changed your mind about something important? Why?

🔆 Who do you know that manages conflict well? What do they do well?

🔆 Who do you need to apologise to for your behaviours in a conflict situation?

Reflections

How to get your team shining

If your team is not shining yet, what can you do? Start with this checklist, assess where your gaps are and take action from there.

Clarity checklist
- *Purpose*: Does the team's purpose contribute to the organisation's purpose? Is everyone aligned and clear on the team's purpose? Does it excite everyone on the team?
- *Objectives*: Is everyone clear on the team's objectives? Is everyone clear on each other's objectives?
- *Roles and responsibilities*: Is everyone clear on each other's roles and responsibilities? Is everyone clear on the black, white and grey of their roles? Have you reviewed this with the team in the last six months?
- *Behaviours*: Is the team clear on which behaviours are critical to the team's success? Has everyone promised to uphold those expectations? Do you have clear activities or actions embedded in the team's routines and working rhythms to embed these behaviours?

Relationships checklist
- *Connection and Trust*: How well do the people in your team really know each other? What activities are in place to

support connection? If there are trust issues, have they been discussed and shared across the team?

- *Conflict*: How often does the team disagree with each other? Does the team share their disagreement with the right people, or behind people's backs? How often does your team align to different ideas and ways of thinking?

On page 242, there is a checklist you can use to score your team's current or future performance in each category.

Where to start if your team is sinking

When people ask me where to start if a team is sinking or constantly swearing about each other and not by each other, I recommend both clarity and relationships. Creating clarity is something that can be done quickly as it's about creating shared knowledge and making decisions. Start with agreeing on behaviours and then work out when and how to agree on the other components of clarity. This will then help the team navigate how to create their purpose, objectives and clear roles and responsibilities so they can do together better.

The four components of relationships are not independent of each other. They cross over many times. To connect, you need trust. To trust you need to feel safe. To feel safe, you need to be able to share feedback. To share feedback you need to feel trusted. And to use conflict productively, you need to feel safe. And trusted. Throughout my research, I've realised it's hard to have one without the others.

If the relationships are poor in the team, start with a connection exercise. Take deliberate steps to create connection. If you start with connections, you start to build credit in the trust bank, which enables other components of strong relationships to evolve.

Leading teams is an art. There are a number of different colours, brushes and canvases one could use or create. The same applies to creating higher performing teams. There are so many variables it would be remiss of me to say the four components of creating clarity and the four components of strong relationships are the only components you need to focus on to create higher performing teams. I have no doubt you could add to the clarity and relationship list – and you'd be right. So if you think there are other components your team needs to gain clarity on or there is something that will contribute to stronger relationships – add them to the checklist. My main goal is to help people stimulate some thinking—and most of all ACTION—to help teams swear by each other and make some sort of meaningful progress.

Cheers
Adrian

PS, I'd love to hear your thoughts, stories and experiences. By sharing our wins and our losses, we can all make our difference. No matter what you do, where you live, please feel free to touch base for a chat, a different perspective or a deep and meaningful discussion on how to get teams swearing by each other and not about each other.

Handy stuff for leaders

I often get asked 'What books are you reading?', 'Which podcasts do you listen to?' or 'What was that video you mentioned?'

To help you shine, I share a number of podcasts, videos and articles on my website. All of the 'stuff' is shared with the intent of sparking some action on your—or your team's—part.

www.adrianbaillargeon.com/handy-stuff-for-leaders

I also send out regular leadership thoughts, team activities and ideas to help inspire. You can subscribe at:

www.adrianbaillargeon.com/subscribe

Let's play together

Throughout the year, I speak at company conferences, town halls, team offsites and industry events to inspire and provide a spark for organisations and teams to do together better. I also run programs for leaders and their teams to help them shine, improve individual energy levels, and help teams establish and implement what they need to make meaningful progress.

If you'd like to discuss how I could help provide a spark, light a fire or release an inferno within your team or organisation, you can contact me on adrian@adrianbaillargeon.com.

Learn more about me at:
www.adrianbaillargeon.com/about-me

Want to stay in touch on social media?
Feel free to follow me on:

LinkedIn	www.linkedin.com/in/adrianbaillargeon
Facebook	www.facebook.com/adrianmbaillargeon
Instagram	www.instagram.com/adrianbaillargeon
Website	www.adrianbaillargeon.com

(Remember, my last name is easy to spell, it's three words: Bail large on.)

Like to share?
If you've got a teammate, leader or friend you think would like *Teams That Swear*, share this link: www.adrianbaillargeon.com/teamsthatswear

Higher Performing Teams Checklist

	On a scale of 0-10, how would you rate your team?	What's one action you could take to improve this rating?
Clarity		
Purpose		
Objectives		
Roles & Responsibilities		
Behaviours		
Relationships		
Connection & Trust		
Pshychological Safety		
Feedback		
Conflict		

General Index

BOOKS

MOVIES

Notes

Endnotes

1   Gallup, *State of the Global Workplace*, 2017.

2   CPP Global, *Workplace Conflict and How Businesses Can Harness it to Thrive*, 2008.

3   RE Potter, MF Dollard & MR Tuckey, *Bullying & Harassment in Australian Workplaces: Results from the Australian Workplace Barometer Project 2014/2015*, Safe Work Australia, November 2016.

4   Safe Work Australia, 'Workplace Mental Health Infographic', Safe Work Australia website, https://www.safeworkaustralia.gov.au/doc/infographic-workplace-mental-health.

5   ibid.

6   Safe Work Australia, 'Mental Health', Safe Work Australia website, https://www.safeworkaustralia.gov.au/topic/mental-health.

7   ibid.

8   T Jay & K Janschewitz, 'The Science of Swearing', Association for Psychological Science website, https://www.psychologicalscience.org/observer/the-science-of-swearing.

9   R Stephens & C Umland, 'Swearing as a Response to Pain—Effect of Daily Swearing Frequency', *The Journal of Pain*, vol.12, no. 12, 2011, pp. 1274-1281.

10 L Carroll, 'Oh Fudge! Swearing During a Workout May Actually Make You Stronger', *Today* website, 6 May 2017, https://www.today.com/health/swearing-during-workout-may-make-you-stronger-t111188.

11 L Lombardo, 'Hurt Feelings and Four Letter Words: The Effects of Verbal Swearing on Social Pain', The University of Queensland UQ eSpace website, 9 October 2012, https://espace.library. uq.edu.au/view/UQ:292899.

12 E Byrne, 'The Many Benefits of the Occasional Swear Word', *Wall Street Journal* online, 12 January 2018, https://www.wsj. com/articles/the-many-benefits-of-the-occasional-swear-word-1515782357.

13 ibid.

14 S Worrall, 'Swearing Is Good for You—And Chimps Do It, Too', *National Geographic* website, 27 January 2018, https://www. nationalgeographic.com/news/2018/01/science-swearing-profanity-curse-emma-byrne/.

15 A Barra, 'Muhammad Ali's 'Phantom Punch' on Sonny Liston Explored in New Book', *Chicago Tribune* website, 3 December 2015, https://www.chicagotribune.com/entertainment/books/ct-prj-phantom-punch-muhammad-ali-sonny-liston-20151203-story.html.

16 *On This Day* website: https://www.onthisday.com/events/date/1965.

17 Safe Work Australia, 'Mental Health', Safe Work Australia website: www.safeworkaustralia.gov.au/topic/mental-health.

18 Workplace Strategies for Mental Health, 'Mental Health Issues – Facts and figures', *Workplace Strategies for Mental Health* website, https://www.workplacestrategiesformentalhealth.com/mental-health-issues-facts-and-figures.

19 N Patel, 'How Loading Time Affects Your Bottom Line', https:// neilpatel.com/blog/loading-time/.

20 University of Massachusetts Amherst, 'Ramesh Sitaraman's Research Shows How Poor Online Video Quality Impacts

Viewers', 4 February 2013, www.cics.umass.edu/news/latest-news/research-online-videos.

21 V Bockris, *Keith Richards: The Biography*, Hachette, 2003, pp. 20 & 22.

22 L Leow, 'High-Performance Teams: A Crucial Differentiator of Business Performance', *Training* website, 30 April 2015, https://trainingmag.com/high-performance-teams-crucial-differentiator-business-performance.

23 S Keller & Mary Meaney, 'High-performing Teams: A Timeless Leadership Topic', McKinsey website, https://www.mckinsey.com/business-functions/organization/our-insights/high-performing-teams-a-timeless-leadership-topic.

24 N Perlroth, 'Tim O'Reilly: The World's 7 Most Powerful Data Scientists', *Forbes* online, https://www.forbes.com/sites/nicoleperlroth/2011/11/02/tim-oreilly-the-worlds-7-most-powerful-data-scientists/#6bcd7ddc602c.

25 A Pentland, 'The New Science of Building Great Teams', *Harvard Business Review* online, April 2012.

26 ibid.

27 L Grossman, 'Nov. 10, 1999: Metric Math Mistake Muffed Mars Meteorology Mission', *Wired*, 10 November 2010, https://www.wired.com/2010/11/1110mars-climate-observer-report/.

28 G Homes, 'A Theory of Human Motivation AH Maslow (1943)', *Glad's Homes* blog, 28 June 2018, https://gladyshomes.wordpress.com/2018/06/28/a-theory-of-human-motivation-a-h-maslow-1943/.

29 J Talebreza-May, 'The Importance of Human Relationships', *The New Social Worker* online, https://www.socialworker.com/extras/social-work-month-2017/the-importance-of-human-relationships/.

30 S Sreenivasan & LE Weinberger, 'Why We Need Each Other', *Psychology Today* online, 14 December 2016, https://www. psychologytoday.com/us/blog/emotional-nourishment/201612/ why-we-need-each-other.

31 D van den Brink in A Hurst, 'How Heineken Mexico's CEO Uses Purpose to Unleash the Power of His Organization', *Fast Company* online, 16 February 2017, https://www.fastcompany. com/3068060/how-heineken-mexicos-ceo-uses-purpose-to- unleash-the-power-of-his-organiz.

32 Harvard Business Review Analytic Services, 'The Business Case for Purpose', *Harvard Business Review* online, https://www. ey.com/Publication/vwLUAssets/ey-the-business-case-for- purpose/$FILE/ey-the-business-case-for-purpose.pdf.

33 N Craig & SA Snook, 'From Purpose to Intent', *Harvard Business Review*, May 2014.

34 J Amortegui & H Darling, '3 Surprising Secrets of the World's Top-Performing Teams, *Forbes* online, 5 December 2018, https:// www.forbes.com/sites/womensmedia/2018/12/05/3-surprising- secrets-of-the-worlds-top-performing-teams/#7759e69140fe.

35 R Kanaat, 'The Harvard MBA Business School Study on Goal Setting', https://www.wanderlustworker.com/the-harvard-mba- business-school-study-on-goal-setting/.

36 C Adams Miller, 'Nano Tool: Setting Better Goals: The Key to True Achievement', 27 February 2017, https://leadershipcenter. wharton.upenn.edu/uncategorized/nano-tool-setting-better- goals-key-true-achievement/.

37 EP Lazear, 'Compensation and Incentives in the Workplace', *Journal of Economic Perspectives*, vol. 32, no. 3, Summer 2018, pp. 195-214.

38 ibid.

39 AP Bartel, B Cardiff-Hicks & K Shaw, 'Incentives for Lawyers: Moving Away from "Eat What You Kill"', *ILR Review*, 16 May 2016.

40 A Albanese, 'Tim Ferriss: How to Rig the Game So You Can Win It', https://www.creativelive.com/blog/tim-ferriss-success-habits/.

41 *News.com.au*, 'Number of Fake Police Breathalyser Results 'Could Be Closer to a Million'', 4 June 2019, https://www.news.com.au/national/victoria/news/number-of-fake-police-breathalyser-results-could-be-closer-to-a-million/news-story/b893267bd0acbbcb53f3c0b20c0c3dfc.

42 Bupa, *Bupa Beat Magazine*, June 2016, https://issuu.com/bupabeat.

43 L Pijnacker, 'HR Analytics: Role Clarity Impacts Performance', 25 September 2019, https://www.effectory.com/knowledge/hr-analytics-role-clarity-impacts-performance/.

44 Adapt by Design, 'Why Role Clarity is Key in Any Organisation', www.adaptbydesign.com.au/why-role-clarity-is-key-in-any-organisation/.

45 SM Heathfield, 'Positives and Negatives About Job Descriptions', 1 July 2020, https://www.thebalancecareers.com/job-descriptions-positives-and-negatives-1918556.

46 M Lombardi, *Gridiron Genius: A Master Class in Building Teams and Winning at the Highest Level*, Penguin Books, 2019.

47 Karolinska Institutet, 'Poor Leadership Poses a Health Risk at Work', 27 March 2014, https://news.ki.se/poor-leadership-poses-a-health-risk-at-work.

48 H McLaughlin, C Uggen & A Blackstone, 'The Economic and Career Effects of Sexual Harassment on Working Women', *Gender and Society*, 10 May 2017.

49 Safe Work Australia, 'Bullying', Safe Work Australia website, https://www.safeworkaustralia.gov.au/bullying.

50 ibid.

51 BJ Rodriguez & R Sprick, 'Why a Positive Approach to Behavior?', *Safe & Civil Schools* website, https://www.safeandcivilschools. com/research/references/positive-approach-to-behavior.php.

52 D Kahneman & A Tversky, 'Advances in Prospect Theory: Cumulative Representation of Uncertainty', *Journal of Risk and Uncertainty*, vol. 5, no. 4, 1992, pp. 297–323.

53 KM Newman, 'Four Reasons to Cultivate Patience', *Greater Good Magazine*, Greater Good Science Center at UC Berkley, 4 April 2016, https://greatergood.berkeley.edu/article/item/four_ reasons_to_cultivate_patience

54 P Lally, CHM van Jaarsveld, HWW Potts & J Wardle, 'How Are Habits Formed: Modelling Habit Formation in the Real World', *European Journal of Social Psychology*, vol. 40, issue 6, October 2010.

55 D Sandlin, 'The Backward Brain Bicycle', *Learn to Change* blog, https://www.learntochange.eu/2016/11/10/backward-bicycle/.

56 J Holt-Lunstad, TB Smith & JB Layton, 'Social Relationships and Mortality Risk: A Meta-analytic Review', *PLOS Medicine*, vol. 7, no. 7, 2010.

57 SD Pressman & S Cohen, 'Loneliness, Social Network Size, and Immune Response to Influenza Vaccination in College Freshmen', *Health Psychology*, vol. 24, no. 3, 2005, pp. 297-306.

58 SL Brown, RM Nesse, AD Vinokur & DM Smith, 'Providing Social Support May Be More Beneficial Than Receiving It: Results From a Prospective Study of Mortality', *Psychological Science*, vol. 14, iss. 4, 2003, pp. 320-327.

59 Psychology Today, 'Self-esteem', https://www.psychologytoday. com/us/basics/self-esteem.

60 J Stendsholt, 'How Peggy O'Neal Took Richmond FC From Defeated to Triumphant', *Financial Review*, 10 November 2017.

61 N Schmook, 'Three Words Powering Richmond', Richmond FC website, 30 September 2017.

62 ibid.

63 J Pochepan, 'Here's What Happens When You Take Away Dedicated Desks for Employees', *Inc.*, 10 May 2018.

64 British Psychological Society, 'The Supposed Benefits of Open-plan Offices Do Not Outweigh the Costs', *Research Digest*, 19 August 2013, https://digest.bps.org.uk/2013/08/19/the-supposed-benefits-of-open-plan-offices-do-not-outweigh-the-costs/.

65 C Jarrett, 'Open-plan Offices Drive Down Face-to-Face Interactions and Increase Use of Email', *British Psychological Society – Research Digest*, 5 July 2018, https://digest.bps.org.uk/2018/07/05/open-plan-offices-drive-down-face-to-face-interactions-and-increase-use-of-email/.

66 JE Dutton & ED Heaphy, 'We Learn More When We Learn Together', *Harvard Business Review*, 12 January 2016.

67 *News.com.au*, 'Commonwealth Bank's Dollarmite Scam Exposed', 19 May 2018, https://www.news.com.au/finance/business/banking/commonwealth-banks-dollarmite-scam-exposed/news-story/21c3e1514981063a6b4fd53276216cd6.

68 S Dowling, 'What Caused the Space Shuttle Columbia Disaster?', *bbc.com*, 31 January 2015, https://www.bbc.com/future/article/20150130-what-caused-the-columbia-disaster

69 A Ferguson, 'Dollarmites Bites: The Scandal Behind the Commonwealth Bank's Junior Savings Program', *Sydney Morning Herald*, 18 May 2018, https://www.smh.com.au/business/banking-and-finance/dollarmites-bites-the-scandal-behind-the-commonwealth-bank-s-junior-savings-program-20180517-p4zfyr.html.

70 *Reuters.com*, 'VW Says Diesel Scandal Cleanup to Cost 2 Billion Euro in 2019: Paper', 23 December 2018, https://www.reuters.com/article/us-volkswagen-emissons/vw-says-diesel-scandal-cleanup-to-cost-2-billion-euro-in-2019-paper-idUSKCN1OL0C7.

71 AC Edmondson, 'Managing the Risk of Learning: Psychological Safety in Work Teams', Harvard Business School, 15 March 2002, https://www.hbs.edu/faculty/Publication%20Files/02-062_0b5726a8-443d-4629-9e75-736679b870fc.pdf

72 R Kark & A Carmeli, 'Alive and Creating: the Mediating Role of Vitality and Aliveness in the Relationship Between Psychological Safety and Creative Work Involvement', *Journal of Organizational Behavior*, vol. 30, iss. 6, August 2009.

73 MA West & NR Anderson, 'Innovation in Top Management Teams', *Journal of Applied Psychology*, vol. 81, no. 6, pp. 680-693, 1996.

74 AC Edmondson, 'Learning from Mistakes is Easier Said Than Done: Group and Organizational Influences on the Detection and Correction of Human Error', *The Journal of Applied Behavioral Science*, vol. 40, no. 1, March 2004, pp. 66-90.

75 M Baer & M Frese, 'Innovation is not enough: climates for initiative and psychological safety, process innovations, and firm performance'. *Journal of Organizational Behavior*, vol. 24, no. 1, 2003, pp. 45-68.

76 J Rozovsky, 'The Five Keys to a Successful Google Team', *linkedin.com*, 18 November 2015, https://www.linkedin.com/pulse/five-keys-successful-google-team-laszlo-bock/.

77 AN Kluger & A DeNisi, 'The Effects of Feedback Interventions on Performance: A Historical Review, a Meta-analysis, and a Preliminary Feedback Intervention Theory', *Psychological Bulletin*, vol. 119, no. 2, 1996, pp. 254-284.

78 B Wigert & N Dvorak, 'Feedback is Not Enough', *Gallup* website, 16 May 2019, https://www.gallup.com/workplace/257582/feedback-not-enough.aspx.

79 D Rock, B Jones & C Weller, 'Using Neuroscience to Make Feedback Work and Feel Better', *Strategy + Business*, Winter 2018, issue 93.

80 R Hanson, 'Stephen Colbert: We Don't Need to "Keep Fear Alive"', https://www.rickhanson.net/stephen-colbert-we-dont-need-to-keep-fear-alive/.

81 CS Dweck, *Mindset: The New Psychology of Success*, Ballantine Books, 2007.

82 Psychology Today, 'How to Take Feedback, *Psychology Today* website, https://www.psychologytoday.com/gb/articles/201103/how-take-feedback?collection=94182.

83 B Wigert & N Dvorak, 'Feedback is Not Enough', Gallup website, 16 May 2019, https://www.gallup.com/workplace/257582/feedback-not-enough.aspx.

84 C VanDeVelde, 'Carol Dweck: Praising Intelligence: Costs to Children's Self-esteem and Motivation', Bing Nursery School Stanford website, 1 November 2007, https://bingschool.stanford.edu/news/carol-dweck-praising-intelligence-costs-children-s-self-esteem-and-motivation.

85 A Huffington in T Ferriss, 'The Time Ferriss Show Transcripts: Arianna Huffington (#274)', 2 February 2018, https://tim.blog/2018/02/02/the-tim-ferriss-show-transcripts-arianna-huffington/.

www.ingramcontent.com/pod-product-compliance
Lightning Source LLC
Chambersburg PA
CBHW071546210326
41597CB00019B/3142